HEALTH AND POWER

THROUGH CREATION

PAUL ELLSWORTH TRIEM

CONTENTS

.

FOREWORD

OH, creature of a thousand moods! Complex of passions and desires, of hopes and fears and of vague, tormenting yearnings! Where amidst all that multiplicity of thoughts and feelings that surge through your mind are you?

Men live on the outside of their bodies, like barnacles. They explore themselves with stethoscopes and clinical thermometers and stomach tubes, with tracts and sermons and political platforms. They grope this way and that, searching for — what? For success? And how many find it? Is there a way which all may tread into this wonder land of the soul, and which, treading, perchance they may find all the rest — success, happiness, mastery, fruition?

The Way exists. You were created for success; for power and perfection of mind and body; for mastery over every circumstance of the outer life; for abundance of all good things. Do you doubt it? You do not. In your innermost consciousness you have always known that you were of the royal household and that all that you thought or did was unworthy of your real nature, of the power and mastery to which you were born. You have hitherto sojourned in the far country of sensual delusions, but even now you are turning your face back toward your Father's house. The Way lies before you.

THE SECRET OF MASTERY

YOU were created for success. I do not care whether in the past you have achieved a fair measure of health and wealth and contentment, or whether you have been the most abject failure in all your undertakings. You have at this moment within you, either active or latent, every faculty and every resource needed for the biggest, most satisfying success you can imagine.

The usual conception seems to be that God, or First Cause, or whatever you prefer to call the originating power and wisdom, created two classes of human beings: thoroughbreds, who were born to win all that they desired; and mongrels, who were predoomed to failure. This theory is just as reasonable as one which would account for the apparent inefficiency of a new locomotive by assuming that it had been made purposely defective and wasn't intended to "work." Instead of looking at it in this way, the master mechanic would probably examine the engine and the engineer, with a view to finding whether the machinery needed readjusting or whether the man in charge was not doing his work properly. Suppose that this new engine was not properly fired, for instance; suppose that the wrong kind of coal was used, or that ashes and clinkers were allowed gradually to fill the fire-box. Evidently the engine would not do its work well and would be a " failure" among engines; but all the time it would have in its very mechanism the elements of success and power.

You were created for success. You were turned out by a master-builder, and within you is every faculty and every form of ability which you can possibly need for the work you were created to do. If you have heretofore considered yourself inefficient or lacking in any way whatever, I am going to ask you to suspend judgment on yourself until you have studied the subject of human adjustment, the science of bringing into activity the latent powers of man, and the possibility of finding and correcting mental and emotional short circuits.

This book is a systematic presentation of these facts, and of the principles and methods which lie back of all healing and all creative success, whether on the physical or on the mental plane. It outlines a definite and effective system of bringing into activity and co-ordinating all the powers of mind and body, many of which have lain dormant so long that they have been forgotten. There is nothing extravagant in claiming that this awakening can be effected: all force is subject to law, and if one man does things which you cannot do, it is because he has blundered or has come by study upon laws which you have missed.

Before we go farther, however, we must clear away a few misconceptions which would prevent your getting at the very heart of this book, which is what you must do before you can apply its teachings. One of the first of these is the old belief in the possibility of one man's learning another's lessons for him. Now, if you and I are to be of any benefit to each other, it must be upon the basis of each of us doing his or her own work. I can bring to your attention some very remarkable facts, together with methods, direct and specific, of applying these facts to your life. But in this matter of application I cannot help you, except to point out in a measure how you may best help yourself. This implies personal effort, but any system of achievement founded on anything else is quackery.

Another possible cause of misunderstanding between us is that old source of argument, religion. I wonder what associations you have with this word. Perhaps they are so disagreeable that any mention of it will anger you. The common idea of religion is of a sort of antitoxin, taken in this life to protect us against possible evil in the next. This idea has never satisfied thoughtful minds, and people of this type usually either have turned away from the religious concept entirely or have modified it in various ways. Some sort of a religion every man must have, if it be nothing better than a religion of agnosticism or general disbelief. Every successful man has a religion, of whose articles of faith he is in no doubt, although he may never have formally recognized this creed in his life. This religion of success will be built up of various laws and tendencies which he has recognized as making for efficiency and satisfaction.

I think that a very good test to which a man's religion can be put is this: To what extent can it be taken into every activity of his life? Is it practical; that is, does it apply to life or just to an indefinite future existence when work will have been done away with? Does it make its follower a better mechanic, or a better merchant, or a better school-teacher, or a better farmer than he would have been without it? Is it a system of living which can be followed seven days in the week and twenty-four hours in the day, or does it have to be put into a drawer while its professor goes to his daily work?

Practically, religion can go a little deeper than this: if it touches the concrete and the visible on the outer side, it will also be found to touch on the inner certain sources of energy and wisdom which, in the hurry and worry of life, have long been overlooked. And so doing, it will be found to supply not only a practical creed for living and working, but it will have silently brought with it from this inner and invisible plane that element of mastery and success for which men have vainly sought without. Accept this as a supposition now, if you like. I will show you before long how to "prove it. And this religion of living and working comes in the end to be the modern doctrine of efficiency, reduced to its simplest terms and applied to every interest and activity of life.

While we are considering the matter of the misuse of some of the necessary words related to living, I want to give you a new definition of sin:

Sin is an unscientific and wasteful method of striving for a desirable end.

Sin does not lie in the thing sought, which, when fully understood, is found invariably to be creative expression. It does lie in the manner of seeking. And so the secret of freeing the life from sin, which is the friction and lost motion of living, is to learn what is really worth doing and then to add to this the knowledge of just how to do it most effectively. "Don't" is the poorest text in the world, whether your sermon is for a child or a man. The people who merely refrain from doing evil without striving to accomplish any positive good are not really living. They are dreaming about life, and, until they are awakened, they are neither good nor bad. A live and active sinner will learn eventually that fire is hot by putting his hand into it; and he is then on the way to learn the legitimate use of fire.

It is absolutely necessary for man to create. The boy who takes the alarm clock apart is learning the secrets of construction; and if he has clocks enough and time enough, sometime he will be able to put them together again. Many men never get beyond the alarm clock stage; they never outgrow the destructive tendency, which is merely creative power used in an inverted way. And the only practical fashion of "converting" these social misfits is to show them how to create positively instead of negatively. You can't inhibit energy any more than you can suppress dynamite.

You were created for success. If you are a drunkard, you can learn how to master appetite, how to regenerate your poisoned tissues and to turn into constructive channels the energy which has gone into destroying your body. Perhaps your trouble has been that you were hampered by what other people called "laziness," but what you knew to be an actual lack of energy. Well, there is the assurance of success for you, too, if you will take hold of the methods I will show you, and will do, rather than just think about doing. There is no lack of energy in the universe, and it is possible for you to come into such abiding harmony with this infinite energy that you will never lack for power. No man is "lazy" or "dissipated" when he comes really to know himself.

Connected with this matter of laziness is the charge often brought against any attempt to utilize the deeper forces of mind.

"It is a lazy man's way of trying to get out of work," says the conservative.

Perhaps so. In the same way, the engineer is too lazy to lift the boiler, so he builds a crane to lift it for him. The people in the office building are too lazy to climb twenty or thirty flights of stairs, so the owner of the building provides an elevator for them. Anything which replaces unproductive labor with productive is worth while, both for the individual and for the race. If, by speeding up the mental machinery and eliminating friction and lost motion, a man can learn to do in a given time twice as much work as he has been doing and to do it better, he can afford to ignore the charge of laziness. \

One other element of possible misunderstanding must be eliminated. Before we have advanced very far into the chapters which follow, it will become apparent that certain habits of thought and action must be brought under control and forced to take their proper place in the life, instead of being allowed to choose their own modes of expression. Some of my readers, I fear, will protest against this very practical application of the theory of self-mastery as an unnecessary hardship. Before a man is ready for success, however, he must come to realize that many forms of expression have habitually received vastly more energy than they were entitled to, and that they have never returned, in results and genuine satisfaction, anything for this energy they have consumed. To be really satisfying, an activity must produce worth while results. Energy which is consumed in an emotional outburst is worse than wasted, for it tends to break down the integrity and harmony of the entire organism.

It will be well to notice, in connection with this matter of self-control, that the most practical type of man to be found in modern life has arrived at this same conclusion, by obviously practical and "hard-headed" methods of reasoning. The modern successful business man, he of the best type, is notably clean living and self-mastered. At the head of pretty much any big and successful enterprise you will find men of this sort: bright eyed, clean blooded, clean minded men, who live simply and work hard and effectually. There has been a good deal of abuse heaped upon these master-workers, for human nature is prone to place the blame for its own failures upon the backs of those who have succeeded; but in truth such a man is nearer the Kingdom than many a morbid fanatic who cloaks his self-indulgence under the various moth-eaten cloaks of conventionality and custom. When the "big business man" learns to see the real significance of his work and to understand his relation to that Divine Mind which is working through every honest workman throughout the universe, he will be a mighty factor in bringing the Kingdom of God, which is the Kingdom of Harmony with a theological label hitched to it, on earth. He has learned to work effectively, and to him shall be added that which he lacks: a broad pity for the weak and inefficient and a supreme humbleness before that Creative Presence of which he is but a manifestation.

In concluding this chapter, I want to offer a few suggestions which may help the reader to get the most out of it:

First, the logic of what I have to say is not intended to be argument-proof. There is a class of people who would rather sit around a well-filled table and argue about the satisfying possibilities of food than put the matter to the test by eating. A skilful debater can prove anything and then can jump the fence and prove that his first truth was a lie. The truth of all I have to say is simple enough to be grasped by anyone who will use it rather than argue about it; and this test will decide many a matter which argument would leave unsettled.

Second, this book is not religious in the sense of being theological; but it discusses from the practical side some subjects which usually are considered solely from a religious point of view.

Third, the chapter following this will deal with principles which must be assimilated as a foundation for what is to follow. The other ten chapters consist of methods of application, and you who read must do the applying. No one else can do it for you. Every method has been repeatedly tested and will work if you work it. The royal road to success is not a toboggan, down which you can slide to your goal. It is simply a way of attainment, insuring success through the directness and scientificness of its methods.

Fourth and finally, if there is anything in my statements which you don't feel like accepting, don't. But don't fight or argue: simply ignore that which does not appeal to you, and go to work at the rest. This is good philosophy. Lies don't need to be fought: they will die of themselves; and the truth can't be done away with, no matter how hard you try to bury it with your protests.

So choose that which you can assimilate, and perhaps the time will come when you will find the rest not quite so absurd. Be earnest and honest. Remember that you were created for success and that your part in demonstrating this great fact is to use the light that comes to you "right up to the handle."

2

THE DIVINE MIND

BY the time you have reached this chapter, there is one protest you will make if you are going to make it at all:

"The world is full of imperfect people. The virtuous ones are often invalids, and the healthy ones paupers. Do you belong to the school that tries to cure an evil by denying it or ignoring it?"

No, imperfection and limitation are real enough. They exist; but — they need not continue in the life of any individual after that individual has learned the truth about himself. Every human being is potentially perfect. Lack and the appearance of imperfection are the results of one or more of three elements: First, misdirected energy; second, dormant life and faculties; third, belief in a set of superstitions which may be called "race lies."

The first and the second of these elements of failure will be considered later. Let us determine now how a man's belief in a lie can affect him. Does his belief change the truth? It does, in relation to his life. The fact is that a man brings undesirable results into his life by an inverse use of the very power which, rightly used, would insure his happiness and success. He is directing forces which he does not understand; often he uses them without even recognizing them, and the results which follow this ignorant use seem to him to come from some malicious power outside of himself.

Before we can understand the creative power of thought, however, we must get back to the origin of things and discover how man comes to be endowed with this wonder-working faculty. The answer to this problem lies in the nature of man himself: Man is the terminal and expression of an inner and unseen life. Back of and within the individual lies a Divine Mind, and it is the power of this Divine Mind upon which man draws, whether he does so unconscious of its existence, or whether he has learned the secret of his own nature and is able to work certainly and scientifically. Assured and abounding success is the result of recognizing this law of man's constitution and of living in harmony with it in every activity.

Nature is another expression of this Divine Mind. Nature is not the original creative principle any more than is man. Nature's work is not always perfect, by any means. The action of flood, pestilence, and tornado is an expression of her destructive tendency, and if this were not at times overruled by the Divine Life, which is always constructive and beneficent, the world would become a place of chaos.

If man is an expression of this Divine Life, why is he so limited in his power of attaining his wishes? The limitation lies in his recognition of his own nature. Here again his thought is creative, and to the extent to which he recognizes his identity with the power back of all life and substance, he learns to manifest power, direct and unhampered.

Let me put this into a more compact form:

Man is a manifestation of a Divine Life. He is limited by his recognition of his true nature, for always and by the very law of his being his thought has creative power. The water in the stream is in its attributes exactly like that in the spring from which it took its source.

After you have mastered this secret, you will be able to see in the life about you plenty of illustrations of its workings. For instance, consider the matter of genius: A "genius" is a man who in whatever line he expresses himself does mightier works than his fellows. If he is a painter, he is a master-painter, and there is an element of spontaneity in his work which can never be added by mere desire or determination. He appears to work not from himself, but from some inner spring of power and mastery. Something greater than himself finds expression through him, and in his humble moments he knows that he is but the channel through which flows a power infinitely greater than anything he recognizes in his little outer mind.

Genius, however, is notably erratic. It may desert a man for long periods, during which he is of the same clay as the least proficient of his fellows; and the work done during these times of isolation from the creative power is no better than the work of other men. Sometimes, too, this quality of genius seems to be a veritable fire of the Spirit, and the mortal through whom it finds expression is shaken and consumed into a premature old age.

Evidently this uncertain power is not what we are looking for; but as the element of mastery and perfection of expression exists in genius, perhaps we may find in it the key to the orderly use of the inner powers of man. If genius is the result of the direct outbreathing of the Divine Life which lies within each human being, why are its results so uncertain, and why does it not work through everyone? The answer is that Divine Mind, like electricity, has Its laws, which must be fulfilled in every particular before It can be brought into orderly and satisfactory expression.

These laws which regulate the expression of the Divine Life, can best be understood by a fuller understanding of the nature of the Divine Life itself, and this understanding will be expedited by splitting the primal energy we are studying into its three basic rays. These rays which unite to form the Divine Life back of man and Nature are: Wisdom, Power, Love. Every action partakes, either positively or negatively, of these three elements; for every action is the full or hampered expression or showing forth of this inner life.

Power we easily recognize in every function and activity; it is that mysterious energy which arises out of the unseen and which scientists have vainly endeavored to explain by assuming that at some point in its evolution "matter," by a subtle change in vibration, became "energy." Wisdom, also, is easily recognized. It is the directing force which guides the stars in their orbits and the blood in our veins, and it is either present in or absent from every voluntary action of men and nations. But Love — love is looked upon as a period of madness which occurs in the life of young people, or as a more or less permanent softness of fiber encountered in sentimental individuals. What has love to do with anything practical?

Love is the most practical thing in the world. Don't be alarmed — the kind of love I am preaching will break up neither your bank accounts nor your homes. It is rather the spirit which may be rudely illustrated by the organization of a big and harmoniously working business. We hear much of "team-work" and "co-operation" in modern life. Well, love is just "team-work" carried to its logical conclusions and extended to take in the universe. It is not a mushy sentiment, but is a practical principle which teaches us to do effectively and enthusiastically our share of the world's work and to turn over to the Divine Life, which is working through us and our fellows, the task of co-ordinating and harmonizing our activities with the universal activity. Love teaches us that it is useless and unnecessary to oppose anything in the spirit of intolerance and that undesirable conditions are changed by a serene co-operation with the Universal Creative Spirit and a recognition of Its perfection inherent in all things.

Now I am not going to ask you to accept this conclusion and all it implies at once. Think it over, consider its applications in the pages which follow, and see if on acquaintance the idea does not become clearer and more practical. These changes of belief are a matter of growth, and all men will grow naturally and easily, provided they accept such light as comes to them and use it honestly. And don't jump to the conclusion that this Love which I am describing will necessitate your giving up your life and desires and going out to be a missionary to the heathen. I said that it was a practical faculty, and so you will find it. It will not lead to a foolish indulgence of self or of others. It is a matter of team-work carried to a little broader application than the ordinary.

Love is harmony applied. It is the regulator of individual and universal circulation, and is therefore the secret of health and of abundance. Any departure from normal circulation in the body is followed by discomfort and eventually by disease. Congestion or depletion — too much or too little blood in a given part — will bring this departure from health. Mankind realizes this, but the thing it fails to see is that harmony of thought, which in its ultimate application is synonymous with love, is the great equalizer of the flow of blood and that those emotions which are at variance with love — thoughts of hate, revenge, fear, lust — are the very elements of discord back of congestion, depletion, and their consequent functional and organic changes.

This same principle applies in the world beyond a man's body. Absolute harmony of thought, which is based on the broad and impersonal love of Divine Life, is the natural equalizer of the financial circulation. Without it a man may experience congestion and have money hoarded in the bank and houses and lands which he has to guard from loss by theft and fire; or he may suffer from depletion, and lack the necessities of life. Neither the one nor the other condition is normal and satisfactory. An abundant supply of every good thing is normal to man, and every man can bring himself into this normal circulation of the universal supply currents by quickening within himself the harmonizing power of Love. He need not wait for the failure of those perennially recurring schemes of professional reformers, according to which selfishness is to be curbed by law in such a way that every man in the land may exert himself selfishly to a certain extent but no farther. These efforts have been made since before the time of recorded history. The only reform which will do away with misery and want is that reform which shall bring into activity within every man the harmonizing power of universal sympathy and which shall turn over to the Divine Mind the work of co-ordinating the multitude of individual activities.

Two practical applications of this supreme characteristic of the Divine Mind can be here made: First, anxiety about the future may be done away with in the life of any individual as soon as he or she recognizes the harmonizing and providing quality of this Divine Mind, and by the awakening of Love comes under its perfecting care. Recognizing the Divine Life and co-operating with It by doing with enthusiasm the work which It brings you to do is the sure way toward a radiant success. Time spent in looking anxiously toward the "future" is worse than wasted, for it tunes your whole being to a set of negative beliefs. The key to the future is the present; use it honestly and earnestly and keep the universal currents of supply flowing through you by the perfect action of Love in your consciousness, and you will not need to "foresee" anything.

The second application is an outgrowth of this: You cannot use the higher powers into whose knowledge you are soon to come to accomplish any unworthy end. A thing is unworthy, or "wrong," because it is not in harmony with the higher life, with the broad purposes of Divine Mind; because this Divine Mind knows that the accomplishment of the thing you contemplate would bring unhappiness rather than satisfaction. Manifestly, it is impossible for the individual to utilize Divine Life for purposes which It sees to be wholly unsatisfactory. Your guiding principles must be in harmony with the purposes of Divine Life — and then nothing can defeat you. We will consider this matter of desire later, and you will find that your real desires are always in harmony with good.

In concluding this chapter, I want to call your attention to the light which these facts in regard to the Divine Life sheds upon some old and much abused words and phrases. One of the most abused of all these terms is the word "prayer." What relation has the prayer idea to the Divine Mind? The same relation that the nervous system has to the muscles and to the brain: it is the means of communication between different parts of one vast organism. Man, the visible expression of an invisible cause, draws upon the energy and wisdom of this cause for his own needs. Prayer is never a supplication to an outside deity. It is the recognition by the individual of his own basic or natural perfection and the acceptance of the good which this recognition insures.

"God." Divine Life is impersonal in the sense of including and harmonizing all personalities in one vast but perfectly co-ordinated whole. This Divine Life knows no anger, no jealousy. The name "God" has been applied to a limited conception of this all embracing life and to a certain extent has absorbed ideas of narrowness and limitation which are inconsistent with the real nature of the Source of all seen and unseen things. The fatherhood of God is embraced in the providing and harmonizing qualities of the Divine Mind, however; and, indeed, all that is good and comforting in the old conceptions applies here.

" Righteousness." The seers and initiates who have written the world's Bibles have recognized the essential scientificness of unselfishness and sinlessness, and have known that through these qualities alone man could find the life of real mastery and satisfaction. This idea of the wisdom-directed use of all the faculties is included in the word righteousness, which is nothing else than "Tightness" or the scientific adaptation of means to end.

" Carnal Mind." This term is used in the new testament and in various metaphysical writings of modern times. Carnal mind is a state of consciousness which the race has built up and in which most individuals are still enmeshed. It is wonderfully subtle and persistent, and no man is finally safe from it until he understands it so fully that its claims cannot present themselves to him in any disguise which he will not recognize. "Satan" is this carnal-minded quality personified; and if we have largely grown away from a belief in a personal devil, it is not because we have grown beyond the possibility of being trapped and brought into great tribulation by that state of consciousness of which the Devil was but a symbol. Carnal-mindedness seeks to persuade men that things are good for their own sake, that sensation can satisfy the hunger of the soul for creative expression, and that a man can gain happiness by sacrificing his fellows.

"Subconscious Mind." This is a modern term. It is the name given to those strata of activity which lie below the threshold of consciousness. Your digestion and the throb of your heart are things which you do not consciously direct, yet it is your life which is expressed in them. This is one phase of subconscious life. "Nature" is the subconscious stratum extending beyond personality. It may be called the "subconscious mind of God." Like the individual subconsciousness, Nature accepts and acts upon suggestions strongly offered to Her; and if these suggestions are unwise, the results, when they appear, will be unpleasant.

We have covered much ground in this chapter and have necessarily put a good deal of information into tabloid form. We have considered the three-fold nature of the Divine Life — have seen that It could be split into Wisdom, Love, and Power. We have considered the nature of Love, and its far-reaching effects in the body and in that greater organism which is called the "universe." In this light we find that Love is the harmonizing element, which regulates supply throughout the cosmos. And finally we have turned the light of these principles upon some of the old beliefs and phrases, and have interpreted them from a new point of view. Don't try to force yourself to believe anything; just be fair and open-minded and do your part when it is explained to you.

3

HOW TO AWAKEN SLEEPING POWER

THE truth upon which physical and mental regeneration is founded may be stated in this way:

The "vitality," or constructing and maintaining life of the body, is infinite in power, in wisdom, and in harmony, and we are that life.

If this is so, why have we so far departed from the possibilities of our nature? The reason lies in that very creative power which we are considering. The man who can build a house can also tear it down. The life which manifests itself as health when directed by wisdom and love, will manifest itself as imperfection and disease when the laws of its being are not complied with. Man is and must always be a creator, but when he exerts his powers without fully understanding them, he is certain to create chaos rather than order.

The visible, tangible, "solid" things which you see in the world about you are always results and never causes. The typewriter and the automobile are results of man's creative power wisely directed. All physical things are results, and it is only the life in them and around them which gives them even the appearance of power. And in its ultimate nature this life is one throughout the universe. It takes upon itself certain limitations, is "specialized" but it never really loses the mastery over matter which is inherent in its very constitution. The life which is now in your body is the same life which created it. It has been maintaining this body ever since you were born, and it is just as fully master of the material elements out of which this physical matrix is formed now as it was before you saw the light. It can never lose its creative power, this life; but, because it is your life, because it is your very self, the inmost and eternal reality of that personality which you recognize as "I," it is limited in its exercise of creative power by your belief, by your recognition of its true nature.

This life of yours in your own body is sometimes called "subconscious mind," because, while it manifests intelligence only limited by the false beliefs which you impress upon it, it does not possess consciousness. Perhaps that seems an impossible combination to you at present, but let it go without argument until you have more to build on. This subconscious life is, then, a specialization of your life, which automatically cares for your body. On the inner side it receives wisdom and power from the Divine Mind of which you are a part; and on the outer side it is open to impressions from your thoughts and emotions. That is where you have been doing the mischief in the past, and it is where you now have a chance to go to work directly. As soon as man is capable of recognizing his unity with the Divine Life, he is ready to begin to use his creative power wisely instead of in a perverted manner.

And so the wise thing to do in regard to this inner life or "vitality" is to recognize it as a manifestation of the Divine Life and hence partaking of Its nature: as being all-wise, and all-powerful, and all-beneficent, just as is the spring from which it takes its source. There is nothing antagonistic in this even to the limited science with which we are acquainted. Medical literature contains many instances of "spontaneous cures," many of them of so-called "incurable cases." Now, these spontaneous cures are simply instances in which, through accidental conformity to the great law of health and healing, the primal life currents were allowed to sweep through the defective organism, cleansing it from infection and from foreign growths and secretions. And what "science" is too blind and too narrow to do, you, who are the master of your mind and body, can do when you are willing to turn within and become acquainted with your real nature.

How are you to do this? By reversing the process which brought you into your present unsatisfactory condition. You have looked at the superficial appearance of things and have formulated a set of beliefs based on this surface appearance. To these you have added other beliefs which were passed on to you by your parents and your acquaintances. Before the time of Columbus, people believed that the earth was flat because it looked flat and because everyone said that it was flat. In the same way you have accepted a set of lies, because they were plausible and because the people about you believed them. Every advance that comes to the world is the result of some man's having the courage to break away from one of these race lies and strike out into the ocean of unexplored thought toward the unseen truth. He has "faith" in something which he has not yet seen, and this faith is his compass.

Before we pass on to a consideration of ways and means of applying these principles, let us consider for a moment the meaning of that word "faith" — for without faith you will accomplish nothing in any line. What, then, is faith? In a book which many of us read in our childhood appears this definition:

"Faith is the evidence of things not seen." This is often interpreted to mean that faith is a quality of mind which enables us to believe something which is not true, but which we must accept and cling to in spite of its falsity. This is often called "dogmatic faith." Now, that is too fine a definition to be perverted in any such way. Edison recently found himself facing a lack of carbolic acid. He needed it for his great work, but the usual supply was cut off, perhaps for years. What was the result? He had faith in the existence of other sources of supply. He didn't see these other sources to begin with, but trusted to the evidence of things not seen. And his faith, like all faith that is backed by wisdom and power, was rewarded. All creators, whether their work be in steel and brass or in words or in pigments, are men or women in whom this faculty of turning with assurance toward the unseen supply is largely developed. Faith, then, is a higher vision which enables its possessor to deal with unseen but very real sources of energy and supply. It is not a blind credulity which believes what it has no reason for believing; it is rather a certainty founded on sight, although not the sight to which we are most accustomed.

So, as you come to the application of some of these principles which we have been studying, don't worry too much about faith. Many of these ideas and applications are new to you, and until you have had time to digest them and build them into your consciousness by the process of growth, don't try to force yourself to accept them. Faith will come as a result of this higher vision of truth, and vision is the result of successful experiment and the assimilation of a well-considered idea.

As a basis for the practical work for which we are now ready, let us state again briefly the principles upon which we are working:

Man is the outlet and distributor of an inner energy and wisdom and love which, collectively, may be called "God" or Divine Mind. Man's success, therefore, will be in direct proportion to his conscious or unconscious conformity to the laws established by his relations to this Divine Mind. Man is the outlet, the channel, and every activity of his life is perfectly performed when he learns to do his part and to recognize the completing and perfecting activity of the Divine Life back of him.

Having come, by an acceptance of his own lies and the race lies which he inherits from his parents, so far from the truth about himself, how is the individual to get back to the logical and masterful way of living? By recognizing and accepting the truth, and by living in harmony with it in every department of his being. That is the whole secret, but in its application there is one right way, while there exist a thousand blind alleys. How is he to "recognize and accept the truth"? There is just one way, and that way has been followed by every great teacher and leader who has broken away from the false beliefs of his fellows and has journeyed toward the light: He must put his recognition of the truth into definite form, and must consider it and meditate over it until it is built into his mind and body. And he can best do this through what are, in these latter days, called "Affirmations." An affirmation is a definite and forcible statement of truth: truth in tabloid form, stripped of all encumbrance and all non-essential thought. There is nothing new in the use of affirmations or statements of truth. Jesus used them throughout his ministry

— "I am the resurrection and the life" — "I am the light of the world." By the use of these definite statements of fact, he helped realize or make real that fact in His life. And this brings us to the motive force within all affirmations:

An affirmation produces results because it recognizes and accepts a truth whose action in your life has been hindered or inhibited by your practical denial of it through disbelief or ignorance.

It does not create a new truth — that is impossible. But it brings you into right relations with truth established before the founding of the universe. You have always been the expression of an inner and infinite or unlimited life, but through ignorance of your real nature you have used your creative power — essentially and eternally yours, through your oneness with this Divine Life — to create limitations, which have been built into your mind and body. You will find them there when presently you turn to look for them. And you will find them very real and obstinate, until you have assimilated the truth about yourself.

Through affirmation, or definite acceptance of its existence, the Divine Life can be specialized in various forms: as wisdom, power, love; as health, efficiency, cleanliness of thought and action, patience, etc. And all this is done by recognizing the truth, which is that the Divine Life manifests Itself in and through you according to your needs; and by denying and dissolving the limited and untrue thoughts which you have heretofore built into your life.

An affirmation may be directed to this Divine Life within in any one of several ways. In the affirmations which the Nazarene used, for instance, he often recognized his oneness with this parent life and simply stated, "I am— " with whatever attribute he desired to express or bring into activity added. "I am the light." In this statement he recognized his unity with the Divine Life and at the same time recognized that this Divine Life, manifesting Itself through him, was wisdom or "the light of the world." At another time he said, "It is not I, but the Father in me who doeth the works." Here he directed the affirmation to the Divine Life in a different way.

The principle to be used in this matter of directing affirmations is to formulate them in such a way as to secure the greatest intensity and sense of definiteness. You can recognize the Divine Mind as the essential life and substance of yourself, and so state, "I am radiant health." Or you can look to the source of all within you as the father of your being and state, "Thou in me art my radiant health." This latter form of direct address to the Divine Mind as the source and maintainer of our being is very effective.

Whatever form of address you use, the principle is the same: We "turn on the current" by recognizing it, claiming it, affirming it; and we direct it toward a particular work by the form of our statement or affirmation and also by mentally seeing it perform that work.

Now let us suppose that you desire to specialize this Divine Life as wisdom or the knowledge of how to act in any given situation:

Make your body as easy as possible, so that it will support itself in your chair or on your couch without the tension of any of your muscles. Shut out the direct light from your eyes as far as possible. Now close your eyes and, turning your attention within, realize that the Divine Mind is consciously present there, as It is throughout the universe, and that by your recognition of Its participation in your life you come into direct communication with it. Now repeat, thoughtfully and slowly, this "key thought":

"Thou in me art illumination, and through Thee I know all things which I desire to know."

Repeat again and again in the same intent and thoughtful way, until your consciousness is "saturated" with this idea. Now turn your attention to whatever you desire to see in the light of absolute truth. Think it over quietly, but without letting your thoughts waver to take in other things. Remember that the Divine Mind does not have to be coaxed — Its natural channel of expression is through you, and your natural source of understanding is in It. There is to be nothing forced or abnormal in this relation, for it is the most natural and beautiful and satisfactory relation in the universe. Remember that it is not the little finite, limited you who is doing the thinking. You have opened your consciousness to the All-Father, and by His very nature as a Fulfiller He is bound to accept your invitation. Don't force your thoughts, but let them "think themselves." If you will follow this method step by step, your success is certain just as soon as you get the knack of holding yourself receptive. We will deal more fully with this later, but for the present remember that claiming the wisdom which is yours, as the expression of the Divine Life, and then accepting it as it is quickened within your mind, is the whole secret of gaining illumination or wisdom.

A few suggestions for meeting special difficulties in connection with the use of affirmations will be useful here. Always remember, to begin with, that the Divine Life desires to work in and through you, and that affirmations are not to force Its co-operation, but to key you to utilize this co-operation by removing your obstructing beliefs. Affirmations are like the tuning mechanism of a wireless telegraph – they bring your receptivity in tune with the divine vibrations. In relation to the Divine Mind, man is negative or receptive; in his relations to the external world, he is positive or formative.

In helping you shut out the distracting thoughts which tend to intrude while you are using this method of receiving power or wisdom, you will find great assistance in looking forward to occasions when the power you are holding yourself receptive to will be needed, and seeing yourself successfully using it. See yourself doing the things you desire to do perfectly and with serene poise and mastery.

A farther aid to concentration lies in repeating your statements with such intensity and earnestness that, although the repetition is silent and unspoken so far as your voice is concerned, you seem to hear them with the inner hearing. This is like distinct enunciation in physical speaking. Concentrate on each word. Realize its significance in the general truth you are considering. Avoid all vagueness and dreaminess of consideration, by regarding intently and unwaveringly the meaning of each word and phrase as you reach it.

Let us consider the application of this method to the bringing forth, or "realizing," of patience. Patience is a very practical thing; it enables its possessor to live the life of poise and effectiveness even in the midst of distractions. Now, if you have considered yourself impatient in the past, just stop for a moment to realize that the Divine Life, or the Father, is love. There is no impatience in love — "Love suffereth long and is kind." And you are the expression on the physical plane of all that the Father is. With this foundation in understanding, repeat slowly and with unwavering attention this statement:

"The Father in me is divine love, and I now manifest His infinite patience and strong gentleness. I am compassion, and I constantly show forth this love-nature."

Now, just "saying" that to yourself isn't enough. You must feel it, must let your body vibrate with the quickening of the spirit of love within you. Let your face picture the compassion you are feeling — and it will picture it if you feel what you are repeating. Forget everything outside and concentrate your interest and enthusiasm on the one idea of love. Half-way attention is worthless.

All of the affirmations which we have hitherto considered have been positive in their character. There is a use for negative statements, or denials, however. We have seen that the subconscious mind is affected by the thoughts which are directed toward it by the consciousness. If a false belief is held in the consciousness and is accepted as the truth, the subconsciousness will absorb it and will, sooner or later, bring forth the logical result of this belief in effects. The length of time which may elapse between seedtime and harvest, however, may prevent your seeing the connection between the two. As you begin to break away from the old unsatisfactory way of living, it will be necessary for you to weed out many of these seed thoughts which you have planted down in the subconscious mind, and part of this work you can best do through denials. In the matter of health, for instance, if you are showing forth any of the so-called "symptoms of disease," realize first that you are a manifestation of the Divine Life and are essentially perfect. Then turn directly upon the intruding symptom and state, "You are a lie of the senses. I am perfect life and substance, and in me is no root or cause of sickness. You are an appearance, a delusion, and by my recognition of your unreality I dissolve you and bring forth the truth, which is always health." Use this earnestly and with concentration. Force yourself to remember the logic upon which it is founded, and don't sink into mere dogmatic assertion.

A time of active work, such as affirmation or denial, must be followed by a period of receptive waiting. This is called "The Silence," and it is the place where the "realization" or making real of your affirmations is completed. Simply sit or lie passive, serenely at rest. Remember that the purpose of affirmation is to key the mind to receive and that your part in this matter is always, in the end, negative and receptive. This period in the "silence" may well come between your affirmations and the time when, with eyes still closed, you turn your attention to the exercise of those faculties you have quickened. In receiving wisdom, for instance, you first key your consciousness to receive the vibrations from the Divine Mind; then hold yourself passive, supremely awake but without formed thought; do this for a few minutes, or until the mind begins to assert its hunger for action; then turn to the things you desire to understand.

One source of misunderstanding I must warn you against at this time: It is easy to perceive the great truth about the innate perfection of mind and body, but this perception is of no practical value until it is so perfectly assimilated and absorbed that it displaces or dissolves all conflicting ideas. Here appears in a new form the old law of seed-time and harvest: your affirmations are carried into effect by the same automatic force and intelligence which are back of the growth of seed and sprout. Your first work will lie in the direction of removing your own antagonisms to the way of living; you will have to tear down the old before you can build the new. You are dealing here with that old problem: "When I would do good, evil is present with me." But it is your own evil. You have built it into your mind and body, and it will take time entirely to eliminate it. Remember, in connection with this matter of replacing the old with the new, that action is the strongest form of affirmation; you must not only formulate the highest conception of truth which you can grasp and repeat it and meditate about it until it permeates consciousness and subconsciousness, but you must act in harmony with this truth. Don't try to preach one thing and live another, even to yourself. The strongest affirmation is positive action, and the strongest denial is the refusal to consider a suggestion or to be hindered or influenced by it. The various "devils," which are race lies which you have hitherto accepted and acted upon, soon become discouraged when you turn your back to them or refuse to see them.

In concluding this chapter, I want to give you five affirmations, dealing with five important departments of human activity. Take time every morning and evening to go over these affirmations, putting particular emphasis on those which you most need.

First, for body and vitality: "Thou in me art vibrant and regenerating health, and I am now perfect in every cell and fiber, in every function and activity."

Second, for effective work: "Thy life in me is power and harmony, and through Thee I do all things swiftly and perfectly.' Third, for wisdom: "Thy mind in me is illumination, and I know the truth which frees from every limitation.' Fourth, for supply: "Thou art my fulfilling supply, and I thank Thee that even now Thou dost bring into my life all that I desire. Fifth, to perfect your relations with others: "I am an expression of the love that suffereth long and is kind, and the strong and gentle patience of the All-Father is manifest in me at all times. Don't ignore any of these, for all have a greater importance than you can see at present; but put the most time and attention on those which you feel you most need. Remember that you are not creating within yourself a faculty which has not existed there, but that you are quickening and bringing into activity a form of expression which is as natural to you as song is to the thrush. Don't try too hard - your part is to hold yourself open to the divine outflow. As soon as you get the knack, you will find yourself showing forth a new mastery and effectiveness in every department of your life.

4

THE SCIENCE OF RECEPTIVITY

SOME individuals have discovered that on awakening in the night, after a short sleep, they are able to see "in a flash" the solution of problems which had baffled them during the day. Others have learned to leave the answering of this kind of questions to the earliest morning hours, when a new wisdom seems for a time to have come into their lives.

All of this is simply an example of the haphazard working of that inner wisdom-faculty created to solve life's problems. The average human being, immersed in mental and physical activity during his or her entire waking time, has to depend upon occasional flashes from this inner light, caught during moments when the tension of outer interest is momentarily relaxed. Manifestly this is not the scientific way of using this faculty.

Success depends upon three sets of mental and physical actions. First, by observation many facts bearing on the work in hand are collected. Second, and most important, the wisdom-faculty takes these facts and uses them as the crude material for executive plans — prepares for their practical application. Third, these plans are carried out.

It is comparatively easy to learn to see and to remember, although there are right and wrong ways of doing even this, as we will see in a subsequent chapter. Any man who has overcome the habit of mind-wandering, however, can gather the material for successful action. But the next step, that of ordering these facts into original and dynamic shapes — this is where genius enters. And the worker displays genius in his work just to the extent to which he assimilates crude facts and turns this material into bigger and more satisfactory applications than have before been made. So we come back to the fact that genius, which is the outbreaking of the Divine Life through the life of an individual, is the secret of all great success. Most truly great men have realized the fact of this partnership in their lives and work of a power greater than they. It is during the times of silent abstraction, of turning the mind upon a perplexing problem and waiting to see what solution the Divine Life will bring, that the "man of affairs" shows himself superior to his less successful fellows. He has, usually unconsciously, learned to receive the wisdom he needs from the source of all wisdom and all "power.

Now let us sum up the teachings of the preceding chapters and see how they apply to this matter of receiving ideas and wisdom:

Every man is created for success — that is, he is potentially a "genius" in one particular line, if he will but find this line. Second, the secret of his greatness lies in the fact that he is the channel of expression for a Divine Life, which is capable under right conditions of working perfectly through him. Third, the initiative in this matter must be taken by the individual — he must turn toward the Divine Life within and definitely recognize It, before It can work effectively in and through him. Now let us add one other fact:

After man has turned toward the Divine Life within and has keyed himself, by the use of affirmations or statements of truth, to the higher vibrations, he must learn to be receptive. In other words, after having called central, he must learn to hear the response.

Now this sounds so simple that most of my readers who have not experimented along this line will imagine it is hardly worth mentioning. To keep still and listen — surely that is simple. And if the silence referred to were merely that of the outer voice, it would be; but the vibrations we are holding our senses open to receive are spiritual, and the silence which opens the way is a different silence than that to which men are accustomed. It is a silence of thought as well as of voice. The seeker must, through patient training, learn to control the thought current, to hold it without strain but without wavering for longer and longer periods, keyed to receptivity along a given line. This is no easy task, and the fact which makes perfection in this matter of receptivity possible to all is that that which he is learning to use is not an abnormal faculty, but one of the basic powers of his mind.

The conscious mind is like a pond into which many people are throwing stones. Our thoughts are accidents, and if we blunder upon just the idea we need, it is indeed a blunder. The reason for this is that we have not learned to listen; we are at the mercy of the heterogeneous ideas which are continually floating through the mental seas, and if we pick up an occasional idea which fits in more or less accurately with our plans, we are "lucky."

In breaking away from chance and luck, the first step is to realize the fact that this matter of getting what we want from the Divine Life is a matter of law, and that law never fails. If we comply with the conditions one hundred times, we will be successful one hundred times in receiving what we desire. Luck is synonymous with ignorance. The man who trusts to blundering into the harmonious use of causes which he does not understand will naturally come to believe in luck.

Now the first thing to do in this matter of receiving is to quicken within the mind the recognition of the Divine Life. We must recognize its "presence within us at this very moment. One of the most successful ways of doing this depends upon the influence of physical action and attitude in inducing mental and spiritual states. Instead of lying down or sitting down and making the body easy at the beginning of this receptive exercise, stand up, straighten your body, draw your shoulders down and moderately back, breathe deeply, and walk vigorously up and down the room. As you perform these actions, realize that the energy which expresses itself in all action is a form of the Divine Life, and that in Its essential nature this Divine Life is unlimited in extent and in power. It is perfect energy, perfect wisdom, perfect harmony or love. Breathe deeply as you consider that you are the focal point where the life and substance of the Unseen Cause meet and that by your recognition of this fact you furnish a perfect channel for Its perfect working in and through you.

A short period of this awakening and quickening exercise is sufficient. Now sit or lie down and make your body easy. Turn your face away from any direct light, and close your eyes. Take time to direct your attention to all of your muscles and to be sure you are not holding yourself forcibly — relax.

Now turn your attention within and rest for a moment, until the swirling thoughts which occupy the mind are stilled. This done, take up the wisdom formula given in the last chapter and repeat it thoughtfully and with concentration:

"Thou in me art illumination and through Thee I know the truth which frees from every limitation.' Consider each part of this formula separately. 'Thou in me" — this is the partnership of the human with the divine which constitute genius, and by your recognition of this co-operation you are establishing the conditions for genius and mastery in your own life. "Thou in me" — not afar off, but in the very center of your being, the gateway to which is your consciousness. Get away from the impulse to "throw" your affirmations into the room about you or toward the skies. You are not to attempt to impress with them any entity outside of yourself, for this Divine Life is omnipresent, and you can make connection with it in your own being.

Analyze the rest of this affirmation in the same way.

With this preparation, I am going to give you the key which eventually will unlock the infinite storehouse to you:

By your recognition of its identity with your life, the Divine Life becomes in fact as well as in theory one with you, in thought and in action. Your mind becomes part of the Divine Mind by your acceptance of the truth; and your thoughts, to just the extent you succeed in freeing them from your old limiting beliefs, will take on the power and mastery of the Divine Mind.

To just the extent you succeed in freeing them from your old limiting beliefs — obtaining this freedom is the purpose of the next stage of this time of receptivity. With your mind keyed to the recognition of its own nature, you are to close it to all thought. This does not mean that you are to sleep or to sink into a "trance." On the contrary, you are to hold your mind poised and radiantly awake, but without formed thoughts. In no other way can you free it from the chains of accidental ideas that habitually occupy it. Turn to your key thought as often as you need to bring your attention back to your original aim, but this time of silence is not to be filled with even the most worthwhile affirmations. You will be surprised at first to find how fully the accidental thoughts floating about in the mental currents have mastered you. It takes time and patience to reverse this mastery, and to come to the point where you can think about what you choose, or can hold your mind receptive and passive, without formed thought.

Following this time of silence, turn your attention upon whatever subject you desire to understand and consider it with serene attention. Don't imagine that the wisdom you are to receive will come as a voice from outside: it is your faculties which will be quickened. The secret of this method is the realizing or making real and vital of the eternal fact of the unity of all life and wisdom, and hence of the identity of your mind with the wisdom of the Divine Life. The faculties are yours, and the increase in power comes, first, from your having by your period "in the silence" cut off all side issues; second, from your recognition of the source of your energy and wisdom. As long as you believed that your power of knowing was limited by the action of a set of brain cells within your skull, your thoughts were limited and cramped by the very creative "power of that belief. The brain is the creation as well as the tool of Divine Mind working in you, and as soon as you recognize the indwelling of this Divine Mind, your brain will attend to itself. The master-workman can always modify his tools to suit his needs. Thought is the cause of the nervous system, not a result of it.

Not everything that comes to you "in the silence" can be accepted or utilized without modification. This is not because the wisdom of the Divine Life ever fails, but because you will not always succeed in receiving the thought currents without modification. Your inner and half-realized beliefs have a tendency to assert themselves and to modify the truth in various ways. You are not yet a perfect lens for the transmission of spiritual light, and "aberrations" from this lack of perfect correction will occasionally result. For this reason you are not to accept with blind credulity, but are to test and observe results. This does not mean that you are to form the habit of distrusting the Divine Wisdom, but that you are to learn, by observation and experiment, just where you fail in receiving, and then to correct the lack within yourself. The time will come when this matter of testing the light which reaches you will no longer be necessary; but first you will have to tear down the old structures of false belief.

Another of your limitations which will at first hinder you from receiving perfectly is that race lie which teaches a man that he is isolated from all other life and that if another gains anything, he himself must do without it. Yes, I am getting back to that very practical subject of love, or harmony. Receiving implies two conditions. The first is an inlet. That part of the idea is easily grasped. The second requirement is an outlet.

Let us take as an illustration of the necessity of these two conditions for successful receiving, the case of a small lake or pond, which, through stagnation of its water, has become foul. It needs to receive fresh water, plainly. And the first requisite to this receiving is an inlet, connecting the pond with a river or other source. But unless an outlet is also provided, the pond as it originally existed will soon be done away with. The vigorous inflow of water will gradually obliterate its banks, and will eventually overflow the boundaries of the pond and spread disaster to the surrounding country. But if both inlet and outlet are provided, the pond will constantly receive fresh water, which in turn it passes on to other channels. It becomes a medium of cleansing and regenerating supplies, not only for its own use but for the general good.

Love applies to just this matter of a perfect inlet and a perfect outlet. It recognizes the fact that no man lives to himself and that if he tries to receive without giving, he will not be successful.

And now I want to state another great fact in connection with harmony, or love.

Without love there is no power, and in proportion as a man loves unselfishly will be his mastery of force. Wisdom is the first step in this mastery, but wisdom is cold and lifeless till love is added. The master technicians are admired for their dexterity and cleverness, but only he who adds to technical skill a wealth of vitalizing and quickening love is recognized as a master.

This is true and practical in every line of human endeavor, from shoeing mules up to writing operas. Love plus wisdom equals power. Love is the master-key, and the more broad and unlimited the love is, the more broad and unlimited will be the power. The man who loves his work, for instance, may be hindered from reaching the fullest success in it by his lack of love in another direction: hate or lust, which are practically denials of universal love, may so wreck his body and destroy his nervous energy that all his professional zeal and mastery are counteracted.

And so we come back to the fact that love is the tuning or harmonizing element in all living and that before a man can receive wisdom or power without fail, he must establish right relations with the inner and the outer by this harmonizing and co-ordinating influence. The practical application of this is that, love being such a master-faculty, its exercise and development should not be left to chance but should be studied and systemized. Get down to business today and have a heart-to-heart talk with yourself about this matter of universal love. Study the things you are doing and your relations with others, and see whether or not you are expressing that broad patience and tolerance and sympathy which will bring you into harmony with the Divine Mind within, and with its manifestation in other forms of life without.

Don't imagine for a moment that this is an impractical thing. You were created for success, but before you can come into the full realization of that success, you must learn and obey the central laws of life. And the greatest of these laws is co-operation. Selfishness is self-destructive, for hate and jealousy and revenge and every other isolating emotion inhibit the action of life, until there is not enough activity left to support the organism through which it is manifesting.

The science of receptivity may be summed up in this way:

Success is the result of seeing keenly, of remembering definitely, and of thinking originally and dynamically, or in a way that leads to masterful action. This quality of dynamic thinking results from the direct interaction of the mind of man with the Divine Life of which he is a part. Such interaction or co-operation is a normal and natural activity, and therefore is subject to law.

The law of receiving is, first, to look expectantly toward the source of supply; second, to maintain this expectant attention so firmly as to shut off distracting thoughts and emotions; third, to utilize the resultant quickening of the power of thought.

The things which oftenest cause failure in this matter of receiving are: First, prejudice, which modifies and warps the truth; this can be remedied by observing our limitations and gradually growing out of them. Second, isolation in consciousness from the Divine Life within and its expressions in other forms of life without. The supreme cure for this is love, which is seen, in its ultimate nature, to be not only the harmonizing power of the universal, but the key to power and mastery in the individual.

5

HOW TO MASTER HABIT

AS each human being reaches the plane of more or less assured and masterful expression in the line of his or her "life-work," it becomes evident that certain race habits which have hitherto persisted have become meaningless and undesirable. This growth in wisdom is the foundation of all true reform, for it cuts the root of undesirable habit, in the desire and approbation of the individual. Until a man sees the worthlessness and silliness of any of these excrescences of habit and custom, it is useless to try to force reform upon him.

In this chapter on habit I want to get down to the practical application of some of the less commonly understood mental and spiritual laws, and to do that I must start at the beginning. For this reason I want to go back to the first chapter of this book for a moment and ask you to read again the definition there set forth of sin: Sin is an unscientific and wasteful method of striving for a desirable end.

The end of every true desire is expression. That is, the real hunger in the artist's soul is to paint with swiftness and spontaneity and mastery. The business man's real desire is for breadth of vision and efficiency of action. The writer desires to master the hearts of men, to make them laugh with him and cry with him, to see the world with his own keen vision. These things are real desires, and because every man is organized for one particular success, every human being has within him both the root of this true desire and the means of its fulfilment.

Now the habits which men must learn to master before they can show forth that mastery in their work which is normal to all, are the results of false desires. The "liquor habit," the "tobacco habit," temper, lust, the habit of catching cold or having grippe or hay-fever — all of these things are founded directly or indirectly on the victim's belief in the desirability of certain things that are not at all desirable when they are understood. And they are all manifestations of "short circuits" in the human dynamo, although part of them are farther advanced than the others and have reached the "seed-time" or result stage. The influenza habit is the ripened seed of other unwise habits. Lust is a short circuit in its early stages, and its results are to be found in other habits, most of which their victim does not associate with their real cause.

The short circuits which we are going to consider are all false ways of thinking or feeling. The man who has found himself and his work does not eat too much, and he is not intemperate. This is the result of his having found his true sphere of expression. His power and mastery are the causes of temperance rather than its results. The fact that many men overeat and overdrink with impunity shows that these things, however undesirable, are not in themselves direct causes of sickness, but are rather the essences which give flavor or individuality to the disease. The real cause of sickness and pain and inefficiency is always a short circuit of emotion, which not only depletes the organism of its rightful energy, but turns that energy into actually destructive action within the body.

One other popular misconception in regard to this matter of health and strength and harmony of expression must be corrected before we can get down to the real science of mastering habit: Power does not come as a reward of right living, but rather as a result. That is, the man who makes a plaything of his emotions and appetites is not punished by an arbitrary judge for his excesses. His loss of power and joy is simply a logical and mathematically accurate result of his having violated a law. The man of keen thoughts and tense emotions suffers more for his sins than his lethargic companion because he has sinned more — his voltage is higher; he is turning into the wrong channels more life and life at a higher tension. It is all a matter of law, and if one man seems to sin with impunity while another suffers the tortures of the damned, it is because this matter of sinning is not what it appears to be. But the law, properly understood, can be followed by anyone; and obedience to this law of being insures power and health and their sequent success.

The habits of feeling and thinking and doing which must be brought under the direct control of the judgment in this matter of masterful living may be divided into three classes:

First come those habits which are purely emotional in their means of expression: anger, fear, jealousy, worry, irritation. These may be considered primary habits — that is, they are the first links in a chain of cause and effect rather than its middle or terminal links.

Second come those sensual habits which are first mental, but which lead to a physical expression: alcoholism, drug habits, and last and least understood, sexual perversion. These are chiefly primary habits, also.

The third class of habits are terminal. They are the results of other habits, but have a tendency to recurrence even after their cause is largely removed. Among these are the hay-fever habit, the cold habit, influenza, sick headache, etc. Many physical causes of these habits have been brought forward, but the fact is that they are ninety-nine per cent, habit and can be mastered by the same means which bring control of the tobacco habit or of fits of temper.

I have mentioned among these false modes of expression the habit of sexual perversion. So much has been written on this subject and so much of both truth and falsehood has been taught that I would willingly leave all discussion of it out of this book. A few things in connection with sex energy must be understood, however, if assured and abiding success is to be made possible.

The central and all-important fact in regard to this function of sex which I want to make plain is that the sexual battery was created to serve two purposes in the human economy: First, the commonly understood function of reproduction. Second, the glandular part of these structures belongs to the class of ductless glands whose secretions or "enzymes" play so important a part in regulating oxidation, digestion, assimilation, etc. The first of these functions is one which in the normal and orderly course of human life would be rarely exercised. The second is a constant and supremely important one.

The next series of facts in regard to this matter is this: Because of the fact that man has come to look to the wrong class of activities for his satisfaction — to "sensual" expression rather than creative — the balance and harmony between these two functions of the sexual system have been destroyed. Instead of this supremely important enzyme being regularly taken up by the blood and lymph, it is turned into other channels, and the body is robbed of one of its chief elixirs of regeneration. The secretion from the suprarenals is capable of supplying this waste to a certain extent, but in nature there is no absolute duplication of function, and the life which is thrown away in false modes of expression cannot be saved except by an understanding of the truth and its regular application.

The gist of this matter may be stated in this way: The sexual system was created to serve two purposes: first, the infrequent one of the transmission of life; second, the continuous and supremely important one of bodily regeneration. The element of sensual gratification did not enter into the original design of Divine Life, and its introduction and emphasis by man results in physical decrepitude, premature senility, and death. That is all there is to the matter, and no amount of argument can change one jot or tittle of the law.

It is one thing to realize the uselessness, un-desirability, and eventual destructiveness of an action, however, and quite another to break that chain of periodic repetition which is called habit. We have considered the nature of false expression — of temper, lust, and periodic sickness. Now, how are these habits to be done away with, after we have finally decided to rid our lives of them?

First we must understand the nature of the force we are combatting.

Habit is the tendency to the more or less rhythmical or regular repetition of certain isolated acts. Now each of these isolated acts is preceded by an impulse, and every impulse has a root. First there are the exterior roots to impulse: the drunkard sees a saloon or a glass of beer, and an impulse to drink asserts itself.

Second come the purely mental impulses — a stray thought suggests the master-desire. Third among these roots of impulse comes what may be termed the "rhythmic" tendency of subjective mind; that is, at fairly regular intervals, the mind below the threshold of consciousness begins to stir and move uneasily, and to send up suggestions toward a certain kind of action. This is habit in its purest form.

The first step toward securing self-mastery is to have an understanding with yourself as to your real nature and the desires consistent with this nature. You can do this in somewhat such words as these:

"I am an expression of the Divine Life, and in my entire being there is nothing that is not derived from this source. Divine Life is perfect in every respect, and therefore in life and in substance, in desire, thought, and action it is natural and normal for me to be perfect. The perfect thing for me to desire is mastery of expression in every department of my being, which includes health, serene effectiveness in my work, and harmony between myself and all other forms of this primal life. Everything that consumes energy without producing an equivalent, or that tears down life and organism instead of building it up, is unscientific. The real joy of life is in working masterfully, in living harmoniously in my body and in the world."

This understanding cuts the root within yourself of lust, intemperance, and all the social discords — anger, jealousy, etc. By it you have recognized your normal independence of all these things. Now you are ready to devote your whole energy and desire to weeding out the seeds and sprouts of false desire.

In this direct attack upon habit, six principles will help you:

First, see yourself meeting temptation successfully, and use affirmations which positively recognize the natural existence within you of the virtue or power you are beginning to build. For destroying the lust habit, for instance, see yourself walking serene and masterful where you have usually fallen and aid this visualizing exercise by repeating: "The Divine Life in me is serene purity and cleanliness, and I desire only that which is consistent with my nature." Use this affirmation as you have already learned to use all affirmations.

Second, foresee temptation as far as possible and be on your guard against it; you know where and why you have fallen before.

Third, when temptation comes, whether you have foreseen it or whether it comes swiftly and unexpectedly, strike first and strike hard. Have ready an affirmation or statement of truth which covers as fully as possible your conception of the positive quality you are building, and grab it just as you would grasp a weapon in a physical encounter. Remember Van Bibber's ten rules for conduct in a fight: Rule one was, always strike the first blow. The other nine he had forgotten, but he found that when he used the first one, the others didn't usually matter.

So don't waste time arguing, don't consider "both sides of the question" for an instant, but start your counter thought at once.

Fourth, if you fail, turn back into the way you have decided upon at once and without wasting time in regretting your temporary defeat.

Fifth, learn as quickly as possible to use the remedy of ignorance, which will be fully described later in this chapter.

Sixth, turn your energies into other channels by going to work.

The third rule of conquering habit was to strike first and strike hard. One of the methods of striking was seen to be through the use of a previously selected "key thought" or affirmation. There is another means of combatting the power of habit which is even less known and which is of invaluable assistance in these pitched battles. It is based upon the fact that every emotional change, before it can become effective, must produce a change in the circulation. Usually there is a rushing of blood to the solar and sacral plexi, and, in the case of anger, to the head. This disturbance of circulation is in reality a very important step in the consummation of the act which continues the chain of habit, and by preventing this disturbance of the blood flow, we can in a great measure check the impulse toward action. But the flow of the blood is not to be controlled by will, you will say. That is one of the beliefs which people accept without test and which is far from the truth. The distribution of the blood in the body can be very easily influenced by the trained will, nor is this exercise one which requires months or years of discipline.

Here is an elementary exercise which will furnish you with the key to the control of your own circulation: Sit down in an easy chair — one with a back high enough to support your head. Place your hands easily in your lap and be sure that all muscular strain and all nervous tension are perfectly relaxed. Now with your eyes closed, direct your attention to your hands. Don't try to see them, to visualize them with your eyes closed, but center your attention on the "feeling" in them. You are usually unconscious of the fact that every part of the body manifests this "feeling" to a certain extent. It is, in fact, the direct evidence of your indwelling life in the tissues, for you permeate your body and are not merely a dweller in the upper story, or head, as you imagine yourself to be. Your life permeates the tissues and by attention unwaveringly concentrated upon the vibratory sensation in any part, you can quicken the consciousness of your life there. Now, as you hold your attention firmly upon your hands, or within your hands, you will find this sensation increasing. With practice you will be able to make your hands tingle and grow warm and moist. This is the fruition of that control of the circulation within your tissues which you demonstrated, in lesser degree, when you slightly quickened the "feeling" in your hands.

Practice this with various parts of the body, particularly the arms, legs, neck, and head. Now consider again the fact upon which the use of this new power is based: In controlling the emotion which lies back of an undesirable action, the vibrations of the plexi must be lowered. This you do by raising the vibratory rate of other parts of the body. As an illustration, suppose that you are given to fits of anger. Now, as far as may be, foresee the approach of such outbreaks — that is, be on your guard against them. But when one eludes your vigilance and gets within your outer defenses, while it is still in the primary stage, during which your scalp creeps and your abdomen feels numb and your muscles are twitching and tense, force your attention away from the thing which is striving to hold it and fasten it upon your hands. If you have practiced the vibratory exercise faithfully, you will be able quickly to divert the congestion of blood from the nerve centers to your hands and arms, and this counter movement of the circulation will break the power of your temptation.

This method can be used in connection with affirmations. At the time you are drawing the blood away from the nerve centers, repeat firmly this formula, "Thou in me art power and harmony." The idea of harmonized power is what you are striving to express, and you will find that the two methods work perfectly together. Add to them the third rule, which teaches you to strike first, to strike hard, and without the delay of a moment; and the sixth, which prescribes an immediate use of the power released from false expression in absorbing and worthwhile work, and you will find that habit is less formidable than you have heretofore found it. The usual effort is to inhibit energy, to dam up one outlet without providing another. This is impossible.

I have mentioned the remedy of "ignorance." This rather clumsy word refers to the power which lies in ignoring something which is striving to bring itself to our attention. The fact of the matter is that an impulse which is not acted upon, speedily dies, whether it is a good impulse or a bad one. The people who doubt this are confusing mental action with idleness; that is, they imagine that because they do not act upon an impulse through bodily motion, they are not acting upon it at all, when they may be acting intensely upon it in that part of the mind called "imagination." A mental act is just as potent in keeping an impulse alive and nursing it along to where it is powerful enough to break through into physical action as physical action itself would be. Wisely directed observation will show you that every yielding to temptation is preceded by a time of turmoil, during which something outside of yourself, apparently, suggests a forbidden action. But — until you give power to this suggestion by considering it, it is powerless. The step between the suggestion of a thought and its acceptance by the will and imagination is so short and usually is so thoughtlessly taken that many will doubt this theory, and will insist that a temptation springs up in the imagination itself, and has to be resisted there. It is eternally true, however, that there is a time in the history of every action when it is simply a suggestion, considered by judgment and will; at this stage it is without power, is cold and lifeless. But, if it is taken into imagination and turned over by that master-decorator even for an instant, it absorbs life and power from us. Our minds have become houses divided against themselves, and the ensuing battle, if it is fought at all, will be a terrible one. The torments of those who are resisting habit comes from the fact that they first let the imagination accept a suggestion of the pleasurableness of an action and then strive to fight against their own life as it breathes life into this suggestion. As a matter of fact, the habit of admitting temptations into the imagination and thinking about them, only to inhibit by a supreme and agonizing effort of will the logical outworking of this thought in action, is worse than useless. Such thoughts poison the mind more than do those which are considered briefly and put into action.

This secret of denying attention to a primary impulse once mastered, you will find that a very little power applied at the right moment will do more than a thousand times more effort exerted later on. If you have built a firm foundation for your change of habit by considering the truth about yourself and your work, and have mastered the secret of vibratory control of the circulation, you will soon recognize in this method the coup de grace of undesirable action.

I don't want to give the impression that even by scientific methods this fly-wheel of habit can be reversed without effort and attention. Self-mastery is not a thing which lazy people can drift into by pressing any metaphysical buttons. It is a matter of study and self-discipline, but it is worth it. As a wise and careful reinvestment of financial surplus will eventually bring financial power, so the conservation of vital energy and its reinvestment in the regeneration of the body will inevitably insure the mastery and power of a superman to him who consistently follows it. Habit does not give up without a fight. The time of transition from sensual and emotional anarchy to self-mastery is usually a time of disagreeable sensations and uncomfortable experiences, and if the lapse from wise living has been of long duration, this transition is not to be effected in a day or in a week. There will soon come, however, a knowledge of growing power and energy, of a new force being built up within.

And this matter of mastering habit is not one for a select few. The man in the gutter can do it if he will begin at the beginning and do his best. Men were not made for gutters or for paupers' graves, and as soon as any human being makes up his mind to be clean and effective, he can be sure that universal law is back of his desire and will help him if he will help himself. There is a certain and unfailing way of regeneration, and no man is "too far gone" to follow it.

One of the most important things in connection with the use of this system of conquering habit is the use made of the time directly after a temporary defeat. These defeats are apt to come, at first, and there are two things to be observed in connection with them: First, get up at once and renew your fight. Second, notice how you happened to fail — just what the inciting incident was and where you failed in applying the principles of mastery. Remember that the fall itself is relatively important, but that the use you make of the period of slackened energy following it is vital. Your tendency will be to "feel discouraged," but the wise thing is not to feel at all, but to think and act. Remember that the tension of habit slackens immediately following such a victory as this, and that you can do much by the right and energetic use of affirmations to strengthen your foundation of self-knowledge against the next assault. The truth always is that you are an expression of the Divine Life, and are naturally and basically perfect in desire and effort. Get back of this and by affirmation and denial proceed to replace the old lies upon which false habit is based. It is neither necessary nor desirable to get out of the world, to run away from temptation.

Learn to know and to realize at all times the truth about life and about yourself, and you will find that temptation is rooted in a mass of lies which you have accepted from your ancestors and your neighbors.

As you progress in this matter of self-mastery, you will find that while habit sometimes comes back with every appearance of its old power and mastery, this is but a "bluff," and that in reality its old-time energy is gone. If you meet it without hesitating an instant and turn all your attention into the wise channels of expression with which you have determined to replace it, you will find that it is but a ghost of its former self and will fade into thin air without giving you battle. But, on the other hand, if you hesitate, dallying with a temptation which you believe to be no longer dangerous, you will find the enemy quickly gaining power and you will have your battle to fight and win all over again. Make your attack on error swift and deadly whenever it reappears.

If the habit you are striving to overcome is largely emotional, such as temper or fear, be especially on your guard against the inductive influence of such emotions in other people around you. Irritation and anger quickly beget anger in those who are brought into contact with these primary currents, unless they understand the nature of this inductive action and guard against it.

In concluding this chapter I want to give you three new affirmations which you may find useful in combatting habits of perverted expression. The first is a statement of the truth about life and body, and can be used to great effect in getting rid of the habit of taking cold or of having "sick headache" etc. Remember to use it promptly on the first appearance of "symptoms" and to consider the statement of truth rather than the symptoms:

"Thou art the life and substance of my being, and Thy life in me is perfect, radiantly effective. Thou art my life and body, and Thou art eternally whole."

The second and third are different statements of the same truth in regard to man and his natural and satisfactory modes of expression and work.

"I am the life and substance of Divine Mind, and I find true satisfaction only in creative mastery. The knowledge of this truth frees me, in thought, desire, and action, from bondage to the lies of the senses."

"I am the life and substance of the Divine Mind, and the recognition of this truth frees me from every false desire."

6

BUILDING A MASTER MEMORY

ALTHOUGH a large part of the subject-matter of this book deals with forces which are beyond the intellect, it must not be supposed that I am advocating a system which will do away with what is usually called "thinking." On the contrary, the man who controls his emotions and who habitually thinks vigorously and logically is laying the best possible foundation for long life and serene satisfaction.

One of the purposes of this book in fact, is to teach the real nature of thought and to bring out parts of the thinking process which are often overlooked. We have laid a foundation for this knowledge by our consideration of the true nature of man. Man is the visible expression of an invisible cause. He is one of the channels through which the Divine Life makes Itself manifest. He is a specialization of Infinite energy and wisdom, and being such, he has certain functions to perform actively, by the utilization of the energy which reaches him from this Infinite source, and certain other functions to perform passively.

In this matter of thinking, for instance, there are three steps: First, seeing or observing facts; second, classifying them; third, adding the enzyme of original thought.

The first and second of these steps, man performs actively; the third he performs passively. Observing and classifying the results of observation are processes directly controlled by the conscious mind. Extending the results of such elementary thinking so as to reach original conclusions, however, is a matter of receptivity. It is built on a foundation of observed and digested facts, but none the less it is not a matter of voluntary thinking. It is the part which the Divine Life plays in our thoughts.

This has been dealt with in Chapter IV and will be developed still more fully in the chapter following this. For the present, let us study the parts of thinking which are more immediately under the control of volition.

The foundation fact upon which all scientific intellectual training is based may be stated in this way:

Original thinking depends upon a mastery of facts; a mastery of facts depends upon memory; and the foundation of memory is observation.

In other words, before you can think you must see. Part of this observing you can do indirectly, through books, but much of it must be direct and original. Accurate and minute observation is a characteristic of successful workers in every line. Some of these successful people are "general observers"; more of them observe chiefly details connected with their work. This suggests the secret of successful observation, or seeing: The mind sees what it is interested in. If you love your work and are putting energy and enthusiasm into it, you will see facts connected with it.

Evidently, then, this matter of seeing will attend to itself after a man has found his work and has speeded up his mental and physical machinery by the methods elsewhere described. The next step in the process is remembering what he has seen, and here appears another significant fact: Interested and therefore close observation is the best possible foundation for remembering. The boy who is a poor speller fails, usually, through simple lack of seeing with interest the words he imagines he is studying. Many very rapid readers are poor spellers, because they early formed the habit of seeing words as a whole rather than as a succession of individual letters. They don't learn to spell because they don't see the structure of words. In like manner, the language student whose whole attention is absorbed by the general import of what he is reading will develop breadth of thought rather than mastery of vocabulary.

And so, when a student says that he can't remember, that he has a poor memory, we can assure him that he is mistaken about himself; and that he will learn to remember just as soon as he learns to see.

As an aid in mastering this elementary lesson of seeing and observing I am going to put into condensed form a system of memory training which will enable anyone to awaken retentiveness.

The first rules in this system are based upon the law that the mind abhors isolated facts. It will hold them — we shall see presently that nothing is ever really forgotten. But often these unrelated facts are so carefully put away that they are not available when they are wanted. This suggests two rules:

First, study facts as parts of an organic whole rather than as fragments. If you are studying history, take one period in the life of one nation and master it. You may do this on a big scale, by going into the minor details and events, or you may study simply the broad and determining movements; but before you leave one subject for another, secure a complete survey and understanding of the period, and of the principal lines of force, the chains of cause and effect, dominant within it.

Second, when studying an apparently isolated fact or subject, use the power of analysis and comparison to bring out likenesses to other things you have studied. In reality there are no isolated facts. Every detail in the universe has some bearing on every other detail. If you will get down below the surface and will find the relations of the apparently isolated facts you are studying to the other knowledge in your mind, you will find memory very hospitable to the addition to your stock of learning.

The next rule in building knowledge into the memory is based on the fact that first impressions are strongest, because curiosity aids in impressing them. It is much easier to fix a thing in your mind while it is new, and interesting because of this novelty, than it is after you have half-considered it often enough to become somewhat familiar with it. And so this rule is:

Third, make your first impression definite and energetic. Never study when your mind is relaxed by fatigue or indolence. Wake up and concentrate your attention upon what you are studying, 'particularly in the case of first impressions.

The fourth rule supplements this: After having secured a definite and powerful first impression, go back at frequent intervals and renew this impression. In studying history, for instance, let us suppose that you have applied the first two rules by selecting a period of Egyptian history, and have studied the relations of its events to each other and to such other historical facts as you possess. The third rule you followed by studying with your mind vitally awake to each new development. Now, in applying this fourth rule, you will find that to make this knowledge fully yours it will be necessary to review this period of history again and again. For this purpose it is advisable to use what may be called "fact books," in which you skeletonize the various subjects you are studying. Put down the important events and dates; write these dates and such names as you desire to remember very plainly. The reason for this will be apparent presently. Look over this fact book once a day, seeing all that you are reading. You will find yourself gradually building information handled in this way into the very substance of your mind.

Another application of this fourth rule lies in supplementary reading: Don't be in too great a hurry to cover ground. After reading one historian's account of a given period, try another. He will put many of the same facts in a different way and will bring out new facts. You will have to read broadly in order to obtain a broad view. This supplementary reading may be done in another way: after securing what may be called a "bird's-eye view" of a nation's history from the pages of an elementary work, take up a more comprehensive account and go through it in the same painstaking way. This is like surveying a land of forest and swamp from the top of a high tree before attempting to traverse it.

The next rule is founded on the fact that each of the senses has a memory or a department of memory of its own. The ears and the eyes are able to make separate impressions of what they receive; and this, added to the memory already impressed by association and comparison, tends to make the record permanent.

The fifth rule, then, is: Utilize visual and auditory memory, particularly in memorizing isolated and abstract facts. Suppose that you are introduced to a man whose name you want to remember: The first application of this fifth rule is to repeat the name so clearly, as you acknowledge the introduction, that it will reach your brain through the ears — as an auditory impression. And right here you will discover, if you have "a poor memory for names," that part of the trouble is that you have usually failed to secure a definite first impression of the name you wanted to remember. Speaking the name distinctly at the time of introduction will correct this.

Hear the name clearly, repeat it distinctly; and next, as soon as possible write the name out with a soft lead pencil; write it clearly and look at it till the form and appearance of the sequence of letters impress themselves on your mind through the sense of sight. This secures the aid of visual memory.

This matter of remembering isolated and apparently unrelated facts is so important that I am going to consider it a little farther. When you start out to memorize a verse of poetry, part of your work has to do with remembering abstract facts. The "sense" or meaning of the poetry is concrete, but the order of words and the choice of synonyms is more or less arbitrary. Many words in the average poem could be changed without impairing the meaning or the rhythm. Your task is to remember the words the poet used; and if you have formed the habit of grasping thoughts and principles rather than the symbols in which they are clothed, you will find this difficult of accomplishment. Many of the "brainiest" men in the world, the deepest thinkers, imagine themselves unable to remember the exact words of prose or poetry. This is because they have not formed the habit of seeing the form, but rather have concentrated all their interest and attention on the meaning.

To insure the definite remembering of abstract facts, such as names, numbers, and exact forms of words, use the power of analysis and association as far as possible. In memorizing the number "4238," for instance, notice that the second figure is half the first, that the third is three, and the fourth is obtained by multiplying the first and the second together. Of course this leaves you with abstract facts to remember, in the end; but it necessitates your seeing the number definitely, and the effort to find relations between the separate figures does help in. the subsequent remembering.

The same more or less accidental relations between names or parts of names can sometimes be discovered.

Get all the aid possible out of auditory and visual memory, with this class of facts. See and hear them accurately. Then review. In memorizing poetry, be sure to secure a first intense impression; afterward repeat this impression every day for a week or a month. One reading a day for seven days will do more to impress a poem on your memory than seven readings in one day. This has been apparently demonstrated by recent experiments.

The sixth rule in developing memory is to use subconscious memory as fully as possible. Subconscious memory never forgets. Down in those reservoirs which lie below the threshold of consciousness is a record of every impression your mind has ever received. Perhaps you have had the experience of dreaming of some long forgotten event and have awakened amazed to find that in your sleep memory brought out details long unconsidered. The fact is that nothing is ever really forgotten.

The first step in utilizing subconscious memory is to recognize it. It exists, and it is a part of you. Don't antagonize it by growing irritable at its "stubbornness" in not immediately supplying you with information you know it possesses. You have so long ignored it that it will not spring into activity at once. Begin now to recognize it and to turn your memory problems over to it. If you want to recall a name you heard long ago and have apparently forgotten, turn within for a moment and realize that the name is there. Call up such details connected with it as you can, and think about them. Then, if the name does not present itself, let the matter go for the present. Above all things, avoid impatience or irritability. Sink the "requisition" for this name into the subconsciousness and wait. In time it will be telephoned to your mind. And as you learn to take this hidden part of your mind more and more into consideration by recognizing it, you will find this matter of utilizing subconscious memory more and more easy.

In the next chapter we will take up the subject of original thinking and will determine just how the crude material of "facts" is to be put to the most desirable use. As a foundation for this study we have systemized the laws of seeing and remembering, which can be summed up in this way:

The secret of observation is interest. We see what we really desire to see, and what we see in this way we have little difficulty in remembering. As a farther aid to memory, association, which brings out the relations between apparently isolated facts, plays an important part. A strong primary impression should always be secured, and this must be followed by review or repetition. Visual and auditory memory should be made to do their share of remembering, especially in dealing with abstract facts. And back of and through all other memory, the eternal impressions of subconscious mind should be recognized, and by recognition should be called forth.

Volumes have been written on memory culture, but if you will apply with energy and enthusiasm the condensed system outlined in this chapter, you will need nothing more. The principles are easily understood. It is the application which counts, and no system or book can help you there. You must do the work for yourself. But always remember that you were created for success in the matter of seeing and remembering, and that by simply doing your part honestly and systematically, you will bring out the perfect memory which has lain dormant within you.

7

THE SECRET OF DYNAMIC THINKING

ACTIVE or latent within every human being is the capacity for powerful thinking. The actual use and habit of such thought, however, is not common. It is not taught in school or college, and one of the most "highly educated" men I ever met had never had an original thought in his life. He was a walking encyclopedia, gazetteer, concordance, and compendium, and his power of classification was well developed. His collection of facts was extensive and well arranged, and he would tell you "all about everything"; but he couldn't apply any of this vast knowledge to any detail of his life. He was dirty, "bilious," had defective eyes, teeth, and hair, and was a failure in everything he undertook to do.

This is an extreme instance, of course, but the possibility of this kind of half-education is very real. Thought begins with securing and classifying data, or information, but it doesn't end there. That is but the preparatory stage, in which the crude material is secured and roughly arranged. The next step is synthesis or extension. That means that out of old knowledge a new wisdom element must be created.

The process of thinking, then, may be divided into these orderly steps:

First, observation, or seeing.

Second, analysis and classification of a fact or group of facts.

Third, extension or synthesis: the putting together of the results of this primary thinking and the construction of inferences, laws, rules of action or of belief.

This third step is the fruition of the whole process. None of the steps which lead up to it can be ignored, but in the final original use of what has been perceived and analyzed lies the reason for all observation. And it is here that the great men of history, the creators and inventors, the "brainy" men as distinguished from the "animal" men, are supposed to be created out of a superior kind of clay. The fact is that every man can think, but few learn how to do so.

"Original ideas" are the most valuable commodity in the world. Every great business is built on the practical application of original ideas. And originality consists in this: that the thinker has seen keenly and has analyzed and classified his material, the conditions upon which he is to work, logically; and then he has added to this commonly available information something which it implied, but which was not contained within it. How did he do this?

He did it, first, by seeing and analyzing dynamically. He put himself into what he was doing and let nothing even distantly connected with his subject escape his observation. Intuition, which is the faculty which introduces new ideas, works best and most surely on a basis of thoroughly digested facts. Having seen everything he could use, he turned within and worked over this thought material until he had discarded the non-essential, the details which were accidental, and had isolated a number of significant but apparently unrelated facts.

In studying a branch of hygiene, for instance, the student would first secure, through observation and reading, as many facts bearing upon his subject as he could. If he was investigating the effect of mastication upon digestion, he would study himself and everyone with whom he came in contact; would notice the effect produced by changes in "chewing" and would study among his acquaintances those who were naturally or by training thorough masticators, together with their characteristics in mind and body. He would add to this the results of studying people who habitually bolted their food, with their characteristics, if they possessed any as a class. From books and periodicals he would secure as much other direct information as possible, eliminating the theories and absorbing facts.

Up to this point, the student would have made use of both observation and classification; but before going on to the final use of this preliminary study, he would, if he understood the working of his mind, pause to complete the classification and digestion of his material. He would strive to bring together related facts and to discover hidden relationships.

And, finally, with this broad and solid foundation of assorted data, the investigator would lean back in his chair and close his eyes and think it all over easily. He is searching for the application of all this information, the law upon which the isolated phenomena are strung. And this understanding of the law comes from the direct interpretative power of the Divine Mind, working in and through the individual. "Intuition" is not a vague or a mystical quality. All successful men and women use it. It is that voice of wisdom and interpretation within which adds the breath of life to the clay of fact. And as the student sits with his eyes closed, thinking serenely of the phenomena he has discovered, he begins to see the lines of force connecting them, the "reason" back of apparently irrational happenings. He has observed, for instance, that where one man's tendency to fermentation and "indigestion" was quickly cured by thorough mastication, another received apparently no benefit. He has eliminated the factor of carelessness by observing that both have conscientiously lived up to the conditions. And now, as he lets the Divine Life think through him, he suddenly perceives that swallowing food in chunks is only one reason for fermentation; that violent emotions will change the secretions, and will pervert the normal action of stomach and intestines. Such interpretative results as this are implied in the material or data, but the illuminating wisdom of Divine Mind is needed to bring them forth.

The first step in constructive thinking, then, is to turn within and seek the interpreting and "extending" power of the Divine Mind, which is always at our command. The next is to test out the ideas received, for thinking is not a matter of accepting untested theories. Having discovered the existence of factors other than mastication in this matter of fermentation, for instance, the student turns this light on the dark places. He "tries it out" on those individuals who before seemed exceptions to law. And so, gradually, by considering, in the light of the Higher

Understanding, the information he has secured, he builds up a definite knowledge of the laws and principles back of isolated, individual instances.

In building up or synthesizing a law or series of principles from a foundation of fact, the thinker must hold himself so perfectly poised that he shall be sensible at once of that tiny voice of protest with which the Higher Wisdom strives at times to turn him from blind a leys and crooked ways of thought. The tendency often is for a theory to "take the bit in its teeth" and to drag the student into an acceptance of conclusions which eventually will have to be discarded. There must be no impulsiveness, no prejudice, in this matter of thinking.

You are not to endeavor to bolster up a false theory. And to avoid this danger, you must not accept a conclusion until it has been tested out on other facts, as far as possible. Try your searchlight on other dark corners, and see if it be really a searchlight or only a flash of coincidence. Carry the results you have reached to their logical conclusions, and see if anywhere they violate the truth. If you find that there is a conflict, don't immediately discard your theory; determine if it doesn't need modification somewhere — perhaps you have not seen it quite in its true light.

The first principle in constructive thinking is to turn within and to seek there the "key" to the maze of fact; the second is to test this key and to modify it, if it needs modifying. This matter of "thinking about" a thing, or of receiving ideas from the idea center within, and then of experimenting with the resulting conclusions is the backbone of thought. Many people use this method naturally and unconsciously. Every human being can learn to think by following these orderly steps.

In the matter of experiment and modification, a supremely important fact is that your mind and its reactions may be used as a sort of standard of comparison. Let us suppose, for instance, that instead of studying a series of physical phenomena, such as those of digestion, you wanted to get at the basic laws of magazine advertising and to build up a working theory. Evidently you couldn't do this by looking into other people's heads and seeing how their minds worked in relation to advertising. Even the answers you would get to questions along this line would not be accurate. But by applying this fact, that your mind is typical of the average mind, in its relations to advertising, you will be able to get at the principles you want.

You can proceed in this way: Take a magazine which contains the kind of advertising you are interested in. Begin at the back or the front advertising pages and go through them, glancing casually at the advertisements. You will find that they divide themselves into three groups: First, those which are neutral, neither attractive nor displeasing; second, those which, for some occult reason, "jar" your nerves and repel you; third, those which are distinctly attractive. If you could really have put yourself into the condition of the average reader, these last are probably the only advertisements you would have noticed. The rest you simply wouldn't have seen.

The next step is to gather the advertisements which you liked and to classify them. Notice in what particulars of display and arrangement they are alike. Decide what caught your attention in each advertisement and whether the subsequent arrangement of subject-matter and display served to strengthen your interest.

Now you have the material upon which to base your conclusions, and for this you must turn within. Think it all over serenely. Certain conclusions in regard to effectiveness in display and argument will present themselves. Perhaps, for instance, it will "occur" to you that the amount of white space is an element of importance; that balance or harmony between light and dark areas is also to be taken into account; and that the make-up of the advertisement should present successive steps upon which the eye can rest.

The final step is to test these theories and to build them into a comprehensive system. Try your theories on the advertisements which repelled you, and see if they violate any principle which you have grasped. Decide how they could be rearranged or rewritten to correct this. By wide and earnest study of many instances of successful and unsuccessful advertising, carried on in this way, you can build a working theory which will cover every detail and will do so logically, because it will be founded on law. In the same way you can master any subject and can go forward from the present common knowledge of mankind concerning it into that uncharted sea of original thought which is always most valuable. Thinking and reading are closely related. The man who is to succeed must supplement his personal observation by grasping the thoughts and facts of other observers. The first thing to secure in reading is a book. The second and third are almost as important. Never read without a notebook and pencil at hand. These are the tools for carrying out what may be called the three rules of wise reading:

First, underline everything of value in the text you are reading, if the book is your own, or copy it if this is impossible.

Second, write down all the original thoughts, suggested by the text but not contained in it. These are yours — they are the result of your own thought, and the book which inspired them is but the steel from which you have struck fire.

Third, after finishing a book, summarize its main purposes, together with the new and dynamic ideas it has suggested to you, and decide how these things apply to your life. Decide what you have learned from the book which should result in action, and plan to put this into practice at once. Reading which results merely in inhibited impulses or in vague emotional stirrings is positively vicious.

In place of a notebook you may find a card index valuable. Or, if you do most of your reading where a typewriter is available, you can use that for annotating and note making and can subsequently file the pages under classified heads in a letter file. Whatever system you use, be methodical in gathering and arranging all the material of value obtainable from your reading.

Your notebook or your card index should be reviewed at frequent intervals. Notes properly skeletonized can be quickly read, and in this way with but little effort you will build into your conscious memory the facts you have discovered. This is not the popular or the easy way of going at it, but it will produce results.

Remember that, with mental food as with physical, it is not what you eat but what you assimilate which counts.

Now as to what you shall read: First, read a newspaper which is constructive in its aims rather than destructive. Many things are true without being of any real significance to you. Never read crime news or reports of accidents. You know enough of the creative power of thought to realize that thought fed on such mental food will not build desirable results.

The weekly and monthly reviews are the valuable channels of news and of other information. In them rumor and scandal are reduced to a minimum, and the worth while developments of the times are treated with surprising thoroughness. Read one or two of these reviews, then, in addition to your daily paper.

Next, invest at least half an hour daily, if you can possibly do so, in reading something "hard." By that I mean something which will force you to follow the context closely, with attention and reason. If you are interested in the sciences, you will find in well-written but not necessarily dry or technical textbooks upon botany, entomology, or geology not only the best of entertainment, but material for thought and for mental discipline.

If you meet many people and want to be a good conversationalist, study history; ancient and medieval history in the textbooks; modern history in the reviews of today and yesterday. The man who builds a broad foundation of historical knowledge will be a broader and keener man in any line of work.

If you are going to read fiction, read only the best. Read Thackeray and Dickens; and among the authors of today, read those whose work is built upon an insight into human character rather than upon plot-building dexterity. If you want to get the very most out of your fiction reading, take a peep behind the curtain and see how the author creates and what his real problems are. Read Bliss Perry's "Study of Prose Fiction" and Pitkin's "Short Story Writing." If you are a playgoer, read Mr. Archer's "Play Making." These are somewhat technical books, but until you understand some of the technical problems connected with novels and short stories and plays, you are not in a position to get much out of them. And you will come back to your fiction reading with a supreme contempt for the writer who turns his art into a box of tricks with which to amuse grown-up children.

In this chapter we have considered the methods and the materials of original thinking. The three stages in this process of thought, we have seen, are observation, classification, and extension or synthesis. Synthesis is the fruition of these steps, for it is the activity which carries us from what is already known, and is therefore the property of every man, to original ideas, which can be the property only of the thinker. Synthesis is the result of observing widely and keenly, and of deducing from many scattered events a law or series of laws; and then of using this law itself as the instrument for farther experiment and discovery. In all of this, the reactions of the searcher's mind can be used as a standard of comparison; any-subject can be approached in this way, and original and valuable discoveries made concerning it. Scientifically directed reading is one of the chief supporters of original thinking and is in itself a direct means of training dynamic thought. Such reading, however, must be systematically and thoroughly done. The man who knows how to read has a wealth of other men's experience at his command, and if he will utilize this knowledge by assimilating it and applying it to his thinking and to his acting, he will find himself possessed of a master key.

8

PHYSICAL RIGHTEOUSNESS AND PHYSICAL IMMORTALITY

RECENT laboratory experiments have demonstrated that animal tissue is practically self-renewing and that it possesses a form of life which is independent of the consciousness or personality to which it belongs. For instance, a section of liver tissue can be kept alive indefinitely in a jar, if it is immersed in a nourishing fluid of the proper characteristics and if this fluid is changed as fast as it becomes charged with the impurities resulting from the tissue's activity. This displaces that old and illogical idea that protoplasm, which is the basic physiological substance, contains within itself a self-limiting principle which insures its ultimate disintegration.

To understand just what this discovery means, we must consider the nature of the human body in its relations to its various organs and fluids. A simple comparison will serve: The body is like a confederacy or union of semi-independent governments, each of which is bound to perform certain duties for the central government, as well as to provide for its own welfare. The central government, on the other hand, agrees to perform for each of its component states certain duties, such as furnishing supplies of food, and attending to sanitary inspection and protection from invasion. The stomach does part of the work of digestion for the entire organism, and it receives, in return, completely digested food for its own support, and is policed by the protecting fluids and organisms of the body, which guard it against the attacks of invading bacteria.

Theoretically, this organization is perfect. As long as each party to the union performs its work properly, health and power are the inevitable results. The trouble arises when the central government does not live up to its contract and either fails to do its police duty or neglects the commissary department. In other words, as long as the organs are protected from infection and are properly nourished, they will go on repairing themselves and doing their work without a hitch.

What, then, is disease? It is the partial or complete dissolution of government in the bodily republic. When the life-blood of Rome became corrupt — when her citizens were relaxed and enfeebled by sensual living — the mighty empire began to crumble. Here and there revolt broke out, or the barbarians descended, and the old-time power of resistance was gone. Two forces of degeneration attacked the empire: first, the civil wars which her own subjects began to wage successfully against her; second, attacks from outside.

All this finds an exact parallel in the history of physiological degeneration. As long as the blood is clean and vigorous — as long as it possesses the power to nourish every cell and fiber perfectly, and to wage immediate and terrible war on any invading organism — the republic flourishes and is immune against attack from within or without. Any departure from harmonious living, however, is followed by a modification of the bodily chemistry; and this in turn produces changes in the functioning of the tissues. Sensualism in eating or in feeling corrupts the government, from the commissary department to the imperial guard. And then the attacks which heretofore have been repulsed so easily that they have hardly been recognized, become formidable.

And as in the case of Rome, these attacks are from within and from without. From within come various departures from normal function on the part of the organs. The attacks from without, like those upon decadent Rome, are made by "barbarians" or lower and more vigorous types of life. These attacks have always been made — germs and bacteria fill the air and the water and even the food we eat, but until the power of vital resistance is broken down, their influence is negligible. This fact will be contradicted by some conscientious people. The defect in their reasoning is that they have taken as their type of "normal man" the average human being, who is far from normal. Normal plasma is immune to germ invasion. Such micro-organisms as find their way into it are rendered helpless by the very nature of the fluid in which they are immersed and fall an easy prey to the phagocytes.

You will observe that this book does not teach that a man can "eat what he pleases and how he pleases" and still be healthy. The average human being has developed abnormal tastes, and if he continues to cultivate these and to indulge them, he is going down to death; indeed he is already partially dead, for death has degrees and not all the corpses are in coffins. The case of individuals who seem to violate with impunity any of the laws of right living can be understood by a study of the chart accompanying this chapter. If any human being were able to violate all of these essentials, he would die swiftly. If he were to live in harmony with all of them all the time, he would never die. Don't gasp — physiological science teaches that if a man can live in harmony with the laws of his being, he will live eternally in the body. Death is always the result of violating law and hence is always "unnatural."

Between the two extremes of violating all the laws and obeying all, most of us exist; and according as we approach one or the other end of the scale are we comparatively healthy or "sickly." Perfect health is the result of obeying all the law all the time. It is very uncommon, because only a small part of the laws of right living are commonly recognized. But, with a broader understanding of the nature of life and of the logical conditions under which it can be perfectly manifested, this abounding and abiding health is possible to any human being who will begin at the beginning and persist in mastering all the steps.

The teachings of this book in regard to health may be summed up in this statement:

Physical health is the direct result of perfect blood, and the blood is the exact index of the rightness (or righteousness) of thinking, feeling, and acting of him whom it permeates.

Organic derangement or degeneration sometimes results from the partial failure of another organ, but this first failure was also a result; when you come to the cause, you will find it to be one of the "roots of disease" heretofore considered. In other words, it is a result of wrong thinking, wrong feeling, wrong acting, or a combination of these. All of these can be avoided or corrected. Disease is never dependent on anything outside of the individual who has it. Germs and bacteria are secondary causes — that is, they may give character, flavor, or individuality to derangement, but its cause lay in a departure from normal in the bodily chemistry, and that is always the result of our own controllable wrong expression.

Evidently, then, the roots of disease lie in those modes of thinking and feeling and acting which are introduced by the element of consciousness. In the following chart these roots are analyzed and presented in an easily comprehended form:

THE ROOTS OF DISEASE

I. Short Circuits.

A. Psychical. (Feeling.)

1. Anger.

2. Jealousy.

3. Fear.

4. Gloom.

B. Psycho-physical. (Feeling plus acting.)

1. Gluttony.

2. Lust.

II. Physical Misadjustments. (Acting.)

1. Wrong food selection.

(a) Partial starvation from deficiency of certain food elements.

(b) Tissue poisoning from ingestion of drugs.

2. Water starvation.

3. Air starvation.

4. Muscular inactivity.

5. Skin paralysis from too much heat in clothing or from overheated houses and too little friction in bathing, etc.

III. Acceptance of Race Lies.

1. Belief in separation from God, the Father.

2. Belief in evil as a positive and sinister power.

Note. —This chart will prove of value in determining the cause of failure to demonstrate perfect health. Glance over it every evening, and notice where you have failed to live up to your part of the conditions of such health. Determine where and why you failed to feel, think and act righteously, or correctly, and decide how you can correct this unscientific expression in the future. If you seem to be expressing perfect health and still are violating some of the laws here suggested, remember that Nature sometimes runs a long account, but that in the end she never forgets to exact payment. She is one creditor who will have her pound of flesh, though she strip you to the bones to get it. And remember that it is much more satisfactory to do a thing because you have decided that it is the wise and reasonable thing to do than because you are forced to "reform" by agony of soul and body.

These are the real causes of disease and imperfection. Even the physiologist, who has specialized so intensely on his subject that often his breadth of vision has suffered, will tell you that anger and expression affect the parathyroid and the suprarenals, and through their effects on these and other ductless glands, produce sinister changes in those enzymes which regulate organic activity. All of the misadjustments in feeling and acting, in fact, are recognized by broad-minded physicians as making for disease. The influence of false beliefs is not so generally recognized, although their effect in inducing various "phobias" and mental derangements is admitted. In the final chapter of this book we will look into these race lies, and determine just where their power lies and how it may be overcome. For the present, remember that the belief that you are an isolated unit, endowed by a higher and mysterious power with a measure of life which from day to day you are slowly but surely expending, will hold you to the old round of development, maturity, and decay, to which it has bound your ancestors. You must get back to the nature of your life as the expression of a Divine Life and build this recognition into your consciousness.

Now let us consider these roots of disease and the physical measures for grubbing them out of our lives. Anger, jealousy, and fear must be overcome by a consideration of the truth we have just stated in regard to the life and body — that we are a part and expression of a Divine Life, that this Divine Life works in us and through us as far as we will let It by recognizing It and holding ourselves open to Its guidance, and that this interaction of our lives with the Divine Life does away with the necessity or reasonableness of anger, jealousy, and fear. Apply the teachings of chapters III and IV, and remember that your work is to tear down the false beliefs you yourself have built and to replace them with the truth.

The antidote for gloom is enthusiasm. Often the suppression of various sensual habits tends to cause a temporary slowing up of the interests and desires. These sensual things have played a greater part in our lives than we have realized, and when they are gone it requires a little time to develop new interests which shall take their place. The only permanent solution of this problem lies in finding our work and in doing it with such mastery and success that our desire for expression will be fully satisfied.

Gluttony and wrong food, or partial starvation, which are given as separate roots, might seem to be closely related. The important element in the one case is perverted desire, however, which leads a man to seek in overeating, or in bolting his food, or in whisky or drugs, the satisfaction which he can never find there; in the other, the cause is ignorance — as in the common case of depletion of the salts in the body through ignorance in food selection.

Lust we have already spoken of. It is a common and disastrous short circuit in the life current.

In dealing with class II, the misadjustments in action, we come to the subjects usually grouped together under the various systems of physical culture, or "nature cure."

The first of these subjects is diet. What shall a man eat to be well? This question has been answered so many times and in so many contradictory ways, that it seems impossible, perhaps, that it can ever be satisfactorily answered.

The fact is that this diet question must be answered by each individual for himself, and as a basis for this self-knowledge I am going, first, to call your attention to four common dietic blunders; and second, to suggest a few of the basic facts and principles which must be applied in arriving at a satisfactory solution. The four great dietic blunders are:

1. Partial starvation, resulting from a deficiency of certain food elements in the diet. A man can starve to death, for instance, on a diet of white bread, no matter how much of it he eats. The food elements most commonly supplied in deficient quantities are the salts of potassium and sodium, the phosphates, etc., and these are found in abundance in green vegetables and in fruits. The salts being soluble, vegetables cooked by boiling should always be boiled as nearly dry as is convenient and served with the remaining liquid.

2. Deficient mastication, "bolting" the food. This results in a loss of food discernment, overeating, consequent fermentation and putrefaction, and the dumping into the system of various poisonous by-products. Thorough mastication of normal food results in the succeeding work of digestion, assimilation, and elimination being perfectly performed (in the absence of 4).

3. Overeating. This is largely the result of the previous mistakes, as a man who is starving for want of certain elements which his food is not supplying, or who is bolting his food, is apt to ingest excessive quantities of the commoner food materials, such as starch and proteid.

4. Indulging in violent emotions while the food is being digested. Anger, worry (a form of fear), jealousy, etc., have a direct influence on digestion.

In order to avoid the first of these errors, partial starvation, it is necessary to understand in a general way the various functions which food serves in the human economy, so as to insure a reasonable supply of the various elements needed by the body in its work of repair, digestion, etc. A rough classification of these is: Tissue building foods, such as lean meat, milk, and eggs; energy producers, such as starch, sugar, and fat; and the salts, needed in the chemical activities of the glands. This latter class is principally found in the green vegetables and in fruit.

The tendency of modern life is to eliminate the "roughage" foods. Our wheat goes through various refining processes until it is a high energy producer, is still well supplied with proteid (for the muscles), but is practically robbed of its salts and of that indigestible fiber which aids in elimination. We supplement this with potatoes, also a high energy food, and with pastry, which belongs to the same class. Meat and cheese bring the balance up in so far as the muscles are concerned. The trouble with this kind of bill of fare lies in two details: first, it is so concentrated that overeating is almost unavoidable; second, it is very poor in the elements of potassium, sodium, phosphorus, lime, etc. The fact that its lack of indigestible fiber renders it difficult of elimination may also be urged against it.

In order to maintain a fair dietic balance, then, we need these three classes of food stuffs. If we have rolled oats or cracked wheat for breakfast; whole meal bread and either a vegetable salad or boiled cabbage, onions, carrots, or beets for dinner, with or without meat; and fruit, soup, and whole wheat bread for supper, all of the bodily materials will be provided. If your diet needs reforming, suppose you begin with some such schedule as this. Eliminate for a while both pastry and white flour products, and reduce to a minimum meat, beans, peas, cheese, and eggs. Don't jump to the conclusion that I think these things are "poison." They are good foods; a little too good, for you are pretty sure to overeat on them. For a month or six weeks stick to whole grains in various forms, vegetables other than potatoes, and fruits other than bananas.

The next thing to attend to is the manner of eating. So much has been written for and against thorough mastication that I am going to ask you to settle the question for yourself. It isn't a matter of argument, after all. During the month or six weeks you have selected for your other test, add to it this matter of thorough mastication. If you are inclined to "bolt" your food, form the habit of sitting down deliberately, with your feet squarely on the floor and your mind off your work. Determine to take time to enjoy your meal. This preliminary determination is the foundation of successful eating.

Next, chew everything you eat to a liquid. If you are eating vegetable soup, chew the bits of vegetable and the pearl barley, together with the whole meal bread you are substituting for crackers, to a liquid. This is an old rule, and it has never been improved upon. You will find that the hardest articles to masticate thoroughly are the semi-fluid things like boiled cabbage. The tendency is to swallow them "whole."

One month of this kind of eating will teach you more about this important subject of what to eat and how to eat than all the books in creation. If you find that it is a good way, stick to it. An occasional old-fashioned meal of white bread, potatoes, turkey with cranberry sauce, mashed potatoes and gravy, mince pie and plum pudding, won't hurt you, but make it a rule to select your foods from the less devitalized products, and to chew. If you are inclined to be too stout, make your abstinence from potatoes and white bread permanent, and put a little extra emphasis on the mastication. "Fletcherism," in its purest form, is excellent for people who belong in the overweight class and whose eliminative powers are in good working order.

Shall you use tea or coffee? If you do, be temperate. There are just as many tea and coffee drunkards in the world as there are alcoholics. A glutton who never touches beer or whisky is still a drunkard. The principle is this: you are to find the joy of life in your work, in mastery of your powers, in masterful doing; eating and drinking were never intended to yield more than a mild pleasure, and to make them the means of intense sensual enjoyment is a certain way of consuming energy. If this sounds uninviting, it is because you have not yet grasped the full possibility of attaining supreme satisfaction through creative effort.

The matter of water drinking properly comes under this subject of diet, and here, too, I am going to ask you to solve the question for yourself. For one month make a practice of drinking two glasses of water an hour or so after breakfast and after dinner and after supper. If you want more at any time, drink it. If you belong to the class with whom water drinking is a lost taste, try it for a month. If at the end of that time it is still unpalatable, and if you notice no improvement in complexion, elimination, or general energy, go back to your former habits.

Now about exercise: Every human being should be so situated that he or she will naturally and in the course of the day's routine get two or three hours of outdoor work every day in the year. Most of us are not so situated; and if we are not, tennis, swimming, boating, horseback riding, baseball, and outdoor boxing are the best substitutes. There is no perfect substitute for chopping wood and grubbing brush and spading garden, however. If you can possibly arrange your life so as to have a little of one or more of these times of direct communion and co-operation with Nature, by all means do so.

Walking is a good supplement but a poor substitute for outdoor work. It is popularly called "exercise," but it is so only in a technical sense. The muscles propel us in walking, but except in hill or mountain climbing they do this so easily that the body is not forced to quicken its various activities.

Dumb bell exercise is also a possible substitute for natural expression in this line. If you have to depend solely upon it, put as much enthusiasm into your work as you can: study your proportions, and keep track of your measurements. Enthusiasm will make anything worth while.

In connection with dumb bell exercise, use the various body weight exercises which bring out the muscles of the abdomen, back, chest, and thighs. For the abdomen, lie flat on your back and raise your feet above your head. Practice this until you can do it thirty times. For the back, turn over and support yourself on your hands and toes, arms straight; now arch your body first down, then up, as far in each direction as possible. For the chest, in this same position lower and raise the body by bending and straightening the arms. This is also a triceps builder. For the thighs, lower and raise your body by bending and straightening one leg until the other knee touches the floor and is lifted away from it. Practice each of these exercises every two days. They bring into activity principally those muscles which are associated with the trunk, and with its important organs and plexi of nerves and blood vessels.

Deep breathing is a natural consequence of muscular work; and if this work is being done outdoors, we have the three great vitality restorers combined in their normal relations: exercise, fresh air, deep breathing. For this sort of breathing exercises there is no real substitute, but if you are shut into a city, you will have to make the best use possible of what may be called the "mechanical breathing systems." They are all summed up in the exhortation "Breathe deep." Lie flat on your back and place your hands across your abdomen. Now breathe in such a way that your hands begin to rise before your chest does. Practice this kind of breathing till you can do it sitting or standing, and you will have acquired the valuable faculty of "abdominal breathing." Practice it frequently, especially out of doors.

In closing this chapter, I want to call your attention to a curious phenomenon, often ignored, which has a direct bearing on seeking health through physical or spiritual methods: There are times of what may be called "low vital pressure," when some little understood meteorological condition tends to bring out all of the physical imperfections which at other times lie hidden. These are the times when epidemics become rife and when the man with the cold habit begins to "snuffle." Usually but not always these are during times of cloudy weather. Often a change in weather is accompanied or preceded by such a period of low pressure, when vitality seems at an ebb.

The practical application of this is, first, not to jump to the conclusion that your system of living is wrong simply because you suddenly lose your energy, or have a headache, or catch cold. Right living in every department of your life will raise you above the power of such negative conditions in time, but you have to earn everything you get, even this kind of reserve power.

The second application has to do with prevention: the instant you feel or observe indications of such a time, throw back your shoulders and "wake up." Your mental and emotional attitude is supremely important in throwing off this sinister influence. Get out into the fresh air if possible. If not, breathe deep where you are, and key your mind to the reception of energy and power through one of the affirmations in Chapter III. Be moderate in your eating, drink plenty of water, and chew your food thoroughly. These measures, if promptly applied, will keep you positive and unreceptive to undesirable conditions.

9

HOW TO BUILD SUCCESS

THE teachings of this book in regard to creative achievement may be summed up in this way:

The same power which, working through Mozart, constituted musical genius, or working through Raphael, constituted genius in art, will work through you in your individual mode of expression, whether that be shoeing horses or building cathedrals; and it will express itself through you as joy, as power, as mastery, as genius. The Creative Spirit did not use two kinds of clay in making men. Every man is created for success; and if he will observe and think and work, he will come to know this for himself.

The first step toward success lies in finding your work. Probably ninety per cent, of all workers "drift" into their final occupation, but a man never drifts exactly where he should go. Every human being is created for success in one particular line, and often in no other. And so, the first step toward success is to study your desires. Stick to your present job, but begin to observe and study your daily actions; notice what you enjoy doing and what you do most efficiently. If you usually fail to do part of your work effectively, find out why. If you discover that part of the faculties which you should possess seem to be lacking or dormant, decide what work you could do which would not require the use of these faculties. For some work or other you possess every requisite faculty in a high state of development. I have known a man to fail completely as a printer, for instance, because his "eye" for type faces — his appreciation and memory of form — was undeveloped; but this same man went into the advertising department of the paper and became very successful.

If your present work is not congenial, look about you for something within reach which would suit you better. Remember, I am not advocating that old and hopeless search for an "easy job." The chance you are looking for is one which will enable you to work harder and more successfully than you could possibly do in any employment for which you were not fitted.

Observe, think, experiment. If you can secure work which these steps lead you to believe will be more congenial than your present work, try it. And try it with enthusiasm and determination. Keep on studying yourself and your job. In this way you will begin to see what you are really capable of doing to the best advantage. Many a man settles down to a lifetime of failure simply for want of this self-study.

Before going on to the next step, let me remind you that only worth while work can finally satisfy the expression-hunger of the human soul. Don't choose for your life-work anything which in your inner consciousness you know to be not the biggest and the grandest work you are capable of doing. And having by honest thought and experiment decided on the work you are to do, hold a council of war with yourself. From every point on a mountain side there is a way leading down and another leading up. From where you now stand, there is a way which leads toward the thing you have decided to be supremely worth gaining. Now, no matter how distant your goal may seem to be, take this road and stick to it. Don't let self-indulgence or timidity prevent you from recognizing the logical way ahead. It may not be the easiest way for the present, but it is your way. There is nothing new in this. Every great success has been built by an indomitable will, which paused only to see the next thing to do and then did it with determination.

The second step in this journey toward success must be taken as soon as you have completed the first: having found your work, master its technical side. A great deal of silly fun has been heaped upon this matter of technical mastery, but in reality technique is just the same kind of obstacle to the inventor or to the writer or to the painter that an axe is to a woodsman: he may cut himself with it, but he certainly will not get far without it. Inspiration is not a substitute for technical mastery, but is largely the result of such mastery.

In mastering the technical side of your work, apply the methods of chapters VI and VII. Observe everything connected with your occupation, classify your observations, find the laws underlying apparently unrelated phenomena. Read everything you can find even distantly related to your work. Read the textbooks, read the technical journals; keep a notebook or a card file in which you store every fact or idea you encounter. And as you read, think. Don't bolt your intellectual food. This is the place to use the power of extension, or original thinking: musing over the facts you have collected by reading and direct observation will bring to you the vision of truth as it exists for you, of your personal relation to your work. No textbook is more than approximately correct, for every human being is an individual, and his relations to all things are individual. Truth is absolute, but our comprehension of it, which is all we can use, is comparative. We can grasp but a fragment, and it must be our fragment. That is why every great creator in every line under the sun has written his own laws of his art; imitators have copied these formulas, but the results which they secured by using them were usually ridiculous.

And so remember that you are an individual creative center, just as all the masters have been; and part of your strength will lie in your breaking away from the conventions, the superstitions, which are binding your fellows, and working directly from your own comprehension of the laws of your art or profession. No two master-merchants or sculptors or railroad builders work just alike.

Having found your work and begun to master its technique, the third step is to apply the modern doctrine of efficiency to your way of working, studying, etc. You must learn to make every pound of energy expended do its share of work, and this means that you must eliminate friction, lost motion, etc. The best time to study your efficiency is at night. Set aside half an hour every evening for reviewing the work accomplished during the day. Decide whether or not the day has been satisfactory. Have you accomplished all that you should have done, and have you accomplished it by a reasonable expenditure of effort? If you haven't, find out why. Review your work in detail, with your consciousness open to ideas from the Universal Idea Center, and you will find things suddenly assuming a new appearance. You will see ways in which you could have done your work more effectively; you will see where things done can be amended to advantage.

You will find it well in connection with this nightly review to make out what may be called an "Efficiency Schedule," detailing the things upon which you are particularly apt to fail. Put in such physical details as mastication, if this is one of your weak places, and consider honestly each evening whether you have done the square thing by yourself in this respect. And include such adjustments as order and punctuality and enthusiasm, if you need to. You can put down the items of this list on the back of a business card.

Following this time of review, plan next morning's work as far as possible. It is important for you to be able to get started without delay each morning, for your energy is increasing then rather than diminishing. In planning in detail the day's work, it will be advisable for you to use a couple of lists of things to be done; one an "immediate" list, whose items must be seen to without delay; the other a "future" list, to be taken up later. Look over both lists every evening, check off the things accomplished, and notice those which are becoming pressing.

Before going on to the next step, let me assure you that this habit of taking your business home with you and devoting to it a little attention every night will not give you brain fever or nervous prostration. Men do not work themselves to death — Bright's disease and arteriosclerosis and the other organic breakdowns to which the workers of the world are particularly subject result from a combination of the causes listed on the chart in Chapter VIII. They are caused by short circuits in the emotions, from lust and worry and anger, combined usually with wrong eating and muscular stagnation. Scientifically directed work hurts no man, even though it be vigorous and long continued.

The fourth step is to master your moods, to harness enthusiasm and magnetism to your work. The wrong use of the emotions is corrosive and degenerating. The right use is constructive and perfecting. The energy conserved by cutting off false modes of expression can and should be transmuted into enthusiasm in work and in the right kind of play. It is useless to try to inhibit, or dam up, energy. It is bound to break through, often with disastrous results.

And so you must hitch your emotions to your work. The steps you have already taken in mastering your profession will tend toward this end — joy in work and enthusiasm for it naturally result from working intelligently, from studying each step and making it effective. Your mental attitude is important, also. Determine to put yourself into whatever you do, to be honest enough to omit anything which you are not willing to do "right up to the handle." And physical attitude has a bearing on this subject of enthusiasm. If you feel yourself getting into the dumps, stand up, throw up your head, and double your arms as if you were trying to show somcone your biceps. Walk up and down and breathe deeply. A positive condition of mind naturally accompanies a positive attitude of body.

Another aid in applying this enthusiasm-energy lies in diversifying your work when your mind seems to be tiring. Don't change too frequently, for it requires a few minutes to readjust the attention every time you change its direction; but don't stick to one line of effort longer than you can work at high efficiency. If you pursue this method of always putting your whole interest and enthusiasm into what you are doing, you will find that your capacity for long continued and concentrated effort will increase.

The preceding rules have applied to your relation to your work. Now you must learn to perfect your relations to the public, so that the results of your ability and creative effort may be properly distributed. The fifth rule for building success is:

Study your market and strive constantly to develop it.

The means of distribution are ready. It isn't necessary for you to upset the present social or commercial system in order that you may reach with comparatively little waste of energy the public you are working for. Socialism and the old community-of-goods idea are matters of theoretical interest. The present social system will do all that is necessary in this matter of distribution, when each individual masters his work and learns to co-ordinate his activities with the activities of the Divine Mind working in him and through him. A perfect medium for the interchange of the products of creative activity already exists, and no man needs to wait for the coming of a theological or political millennium before he can begin to work masterfully and to reap the full reward of his working.

"What are we to do with our competitors?

First, study them; study their methods of work and the results they are securing.

Second, try to co-operate with them; do your share in building up that guild spirit which enables all the workers in one line to harmonize their efforts and so to eliminate much lost motion. This is the scientific side of both unionism and the trust movement, and however fully other sides of these activities may eventually be curbed, this spirit of united and harmonious effort is destined to increase.

The third thing to do with your competitors is to forget them. Kick the word competition out of your vocabulary. It is based on the assumption that men are created with interchangeable minds, and is therefore a lie. You have no competitors and can have none, for you are an individual; and if you will let It, the Divine Life will express Itself through you in a new and original way.

This brings us to what I should call the Great Principle in all successful business: Develop the latent markets for your goods. Study the fine art of advertising. Remember that when you have laid your foundation by mastering the technique of your profession or business and have eliminated friction from your methods of work, it is your duty to reach as big a circle as possible of those who can use your goods.

There is nothing selfish in this; it is educational. When you teach a man to be dissatisfied with lack and to desire the better things of life, you are giving him an impulse toward self-development. The man with the hoe is the man whose desires are crude and imperfectly developed. He wants a crust and a corner in a hovel. It is your duty to teach him to want good food, and a bungalow, and sanitary furniture, and a phonograph. Go after the undeveloped business.

Another important rule is: Develop your magnetism. Bring into activity the qualities within yourself which make men want to buy from you. If you will study your attitude toward the people with whom you deal, you will find that some of them leave you with "a good taste in your mouth." You have felt a tingling exhilaration in their presence, have liked them and their methods, and have been predisposed in favor of the goods they offered you. This kind of magnetism has nothing to do with "hypnotism." The men who are truly magnetic would laugh at the idea of controlling others in any such way.

The real secret of magnetism is three-fold: It depends, first, upon sincere kindliness — the most magnetic men in the world are the "good fellows" who are always willing to put themselves out for a friend and who number among their friends pretty nearly everyone they meet.

The second requisite to magnetism is that sincere belief in your goods and in yourself which results in self-confidence.

The third requisite is vitality, "punch," a generous supply of reserve power. Good salesmen are almost invariably highly endowed with nervous energy.

To sum up: The kind of magnetism which makes people want to buy your goods is built on a broad and deep love of people, and on love and mastery of your work, and on vital energy. And any man can become "magnetic" if he is willing to pay the price.

Having mastered your work, developed all the possible markets for it, and brought out within yourself those broad qualities which eliminate the resistance of the buying public, it will be necessary for you to go a step farther: After you have sold a man anything, from a grindstone to a poem, see to it that he is satisfied with his bargain. The day of sharp bargains is past. The modern idea is "service," service to the man who has spent his money with you. And this service idea, being based on the Golden Rule, is one of the greatest and most successful developments of the twentieth century. The old belief was that anything which would "get the money" was good enough. The modern selling organization knows that it is the "repeat orders" and the satisfied customers which furnish the real horse-power of business.

And so this rule may be recapitulated: "Give the customer value received for every penny, and see that he knows he is getting his money's worth. Education does not end with teaching people to buy goods. You must often teach them how to use what they have bought, how to get the most satisfaction out of the instrument of satisfaction you have sold them.

And now, having completed the circle, we reach again the text stated at the beginning of this chapter: The creative spirit did not use two kinds of clay in making men. Every human being is created for success and if he will observe and think and work, he will come to know this for himself. The first step in this direction lies in finding his work; the second in mastering it; and the third in distributing it to the consumer without waste of effort or material. Success is not a place at which he is to arrive and stop: it is a way of going forward, is mastery rather than mere possession of any physical thing.

And finally, having taken time thoughtfully to consider your situation and to choose the most promising means for bettering it, remember that the efforts you are putting forth are in harmony with the desire of Divine Mind, which is always for you to succeed, provided you are seeking real success. And this being so, the chances which you can see of things "happening" favorably or otherwise for your purposes are not really chances at all, but are certainties of a favorable issue, unless a better solution of your problem is working itself out.

Recognize the interworking of the Divine Life with yours. Dreamy philosophers often make the mistake of trying to replace work and purposeful thinking with "affirmations" or prayers of various sorts. Prayer was never intended to suspend the working of the laws of cause and effect, and Infinite Life itself is powerless to help you until you have done your own part. But, having laid your foundation as outlined in this chapter, it is of supreme importance that you realize your relations with this Primal Life and Wisdom working in and through you. Such a recognition will make you positive, dynamic, invincible.

Use this affirmation or key thought, realizing as you use it that by your recognition and acceptance of the Infinite Life you are opening the way for It to manifest Itself purposefully and perfectly in your life, instead of intermittently, as before:

"Thy life in me is abounding success, and through Thee I am master of every event and circumstance which affects me."

Use this as if the whole responsibility for your success or failure rested with the Unseen. Then go about your work as if it all rested with you. This is the partnership of the human with the divine which is destined to create a new heaven by creating a new earth.

10

THE THREE PLANES OF HEALING

HEALTH is the normal attribute of normal man. Disease is the condition of imperfect functioning resulting from man's endeavor to defy the laws of his being. Healing is the process of readjustment which brings the individual back into harmony with these laws of life.

Animal man is governed largely by instinct. The laws of life, as they relate to him, are vastly more simple than are those laws which bind intellectual man. And for this reason animal man is usually "healthy" during the years of his prime. He lives crudely and selfishly, but he is organized for crude, selfish living. His appetites are vigorous, and he relishes an abundance of plain, coarse food. Instinct leads him to select those conditions of living which are best for him.

Intellectual man has lost the attribute of instinct and has not yet reached the stage where intuition guides him. Social and moral laws are beginning to exert their power — he is no longer an individual, but one of the multitude of parts which, collectively, constitute society. And for this reason the crude and selfish living of animal man no longer suffices to maintain him in health. The law has not changed, but he has passed out of the primary grade of living, and must readjust himself and his habits.

Healing is readjustment. Health is not a thing which may be obtained out of bottles or pill boxes. It is simply and always the harmonious working of the human machine when the laws of its being are complied with. Every ailing man or woman in the universe can be " healed," provided he or she finds the in-harmony which is at the root of his or her disease and corrects it.

Healing is readjustment; and because the men and women about us are not all living on the same plane of development, it is impossible to lay down a course of "treatment" which will cure every case of sickness. When animal man, one of the crude and simply organized type, does get out of adjustment and begins to show forth symptoms of disease, his healing is usually to be accomplished by a simple change in diet or of some of the other physical habits. The student, the professional man, the artist, on the other hand, often spends years in futilely experimenting with one "diet" after another. He has lost the guiding power of instinct and often clings blindly to the very habits which are killing him. The readjustments which will heal him must include more than physical details; his emotions and his thoughts are intense and concentrated, and unless these are brought into harmony with truth, they will tear down his physical mechanism more swiftly than any physical system of healing can build it up.

It is because of this complex nature of the healing art that many "schools" have sprung up, throughout the ages, and have flourished for a time, only to be superseded by others. The final development of "physical healing" has brought us the physician of today — and already the more advanced and open-minded of his fraternity are seeing the handwriting on the wall. In these latter days the medical fraternity is divided into two camps, one of which openly advocates what may be called "natural treatment," which consists in making such physical readjustments as are obviously needed — changes in ventilation, diet, exercise, etc. — and then "letting Nature take her course." The other is experimenting frantically and fanatically with serums and antitoxins. The drugs of yesterday are all but gone. Serum-therapy is the recognized order with "up-to-date" doctors.

And now, before we turn to a consideration of the logical methods of readjustment which are back of cure, let me speak one word more concerning the modern physician, if you still believe in him; or, if you "believe" in New Thought but let your attitude end with belief. If you are determined to lead a crude and selfish existence, are determined not to make those changes which will bring you into harmony with the law of love and regeneration — it will be far better for you to stick to your "doctor." It is all a matter of willingness to pay the price. If you will not live by the law of regeneration, don't lie to yourself. Be one thing or the other. And if you decide that the gain is not worth the sacrifice of your selfish "pleasures," if you cannot yet find supreme joy in creative mastery and expression, give your doctor a chance. Don't wait till you are sick to consult him — go regularly every six months and have yourself examined; let him test your "blood pressure" and the condition of your secretions. He regards you as a sort of walking test tube, and to do his work even passably, he must be allowed to experiment with you at frequent intervals. And in the meantime, prepare for the worst, for no system which depends upon artificial methods of quickening the healing reactions of "Nature," can bring more than temporary relief.

If, on the other hand, you elect to turn away from the shadow of healing toward the reality, make up your mind to go at it with unswerving fidelity. Determine to let no guilty thought or action escape. In other words, choose the system you are prepared to support with your manner of living, and then do so consistently.

Most systems of healing are fractional; that is, they take into consideration only a part of the readjustments which must be made to insure health. Remember that healing is readjustment. Consider, as an illustration, the case of a gasoline engine which fails to do its work. An expert is called in, and being a man who recognizes just one set of engine troubles, he promptly prescribes: "Your batteries are weak. You must renew them, so that you get a hot spark for your ignition." The batteries are changed, but still the engine refuses to go. "It's an incurable case," says the expert. "We've done all that human power can do — this engine is doomed!"

This is fractional healing. If this expert had been called in in a case where the ignition was really at fault, he would have produced a "cure." In this case, perhaps the carburetor needs adjusting or a needle valve has become clogged. To cure the engine every time, a complete system of healing must be employed — one which will recognize all the misadjustments to which engines are subject, and which understands the correction for each.

Now, the human engine is more complex than any other mechanism. It is subject to many misadjustments, and the only system which will always result in a "cure," is that complete system which takes into account all of these misadjustments. That is why physical culture and many schools of mental science sometimes succeed and often fail. They are fractional — physical culture, for instance, blunders upon many cases of sickness where the principal misadjustment is in eating or breathing and where a correction of the habits involved in these functions is sufficient to bring about at least temporary relief. But physical culture does not recognize the need of scientific thinking and feeling, and is therefore powerless to help that multitude of sufferers who are the victims of false thought or perverted emotions.

Whether you are striving to heal yourself or another, the first thing to do is to "diagnose" the case, to find the principal misadjustments which must be corrected to insure a return to the normal, which is always health. The chart of disease roots given in Chapter VIII will prove of great value in this work of diagnosis. Open yourself to the guiding wisdom of the Father within, then consider honestly and earnestly the various causes of inharmony. And, let me repeat, do this honestly. Remember, you are now considering the shortcomings of the personal man who has brought all your trouble to you. He has sinned in various ways, or you would never have known inharmony. It is necessary for you to locate these moral and mental adhesions and sore spots, so that you can correct them. Cast behind you the rubbish of "inherited weakness" and "constitutional predisposition." Stand on your feet and be honest in this self-scrutiny. Decide honestly and earnestly where you have fallen short in the past, and make out a schedule, a definite and complete formula, which shall insure your correcting these misadjustments.

The false habits listed in class II are apt to be neglected by New Thought teachers and healers. Don't make this mistake — before you can come to the place where your body will be beyond the compulsion of these lower laws, you will have to earn your freedom by obedience. It is easier to work many problems by algebra than by arithmetic, but arithmetic must be mastered first. The time will come, probably, when you will not need to exercise your muscles or to consider the scientific adaptation of your food to your bodily needs. At present there is a very real need for your understanding and observing to the letter the simple laws of physical righteousness. These readjustments made, you can go on to the next series, certain that you have built a foundation for healing.

The psychical and psycho-physical misadjustments are more difficult to deal with, but we have already considered the ways and means of mastering habit. Get down to business, and don't imagine that "Nature" will forgive you if you continue to violate her laws. She will forgive you for your past sins, provided you have done with all of them now. Healing is readjustment, not hocus-pocus. There is no magic for permanently defying law, and if you insist on trying to guard and preserve your fits of temper, or your lust, or your impatience, you will have to pay the price in impaired efficiency and eventually in physical agony.

Now let us consider the third class of misadjustments. These are individual and race beliefs, first, in separation from Infinite Life; second, in the existence of evil as a positive, malignant force. If you make all of the readjustments in living scheduled under I and II, but fail to root out these race lies, you will live long and happily — but you will go down the grade of diminishing vitality to ultimate somatic death. Study the writings of Cornaro. This Italian gentleman seems to have made most of the corrections in the first two divisions of our schedule, but always he is looking forward to the time when death from old age, from the exhaustion of the vital "humors" in his body, shall take him to an existence of bliss. He missed this point, and his belief in separation from the Father and in the existence of death as an actual disintegrating process, eventually bore its logical fruit.

To the man who is showing forth the symptoms of any well-recognized "disease," this belief in separation and evil is a very real and a very terrible thing. The word "tuberculosis" is one of the most dangerous factors in bringing about a complete readjustment in many cases. The "invalids" have stamped this label on themselves, and are well acquainted with the usual classical symptoms and termination. Bright's disease, heart trouble — all of these bugaboos frighten people into their graves every day of the year. The dynamic belief in a disease paralyzes resistance. And so, with the foundation of right living and feeling established, the next thing to do is to begin to grow new beliefs, new mental patterns, in place of the race lies which have been built into the mind. And this is the most difficult readjustment of all.

The first step in getting back to the truth is to think over the basic facts concerning your relation to Infinite Life. You are a manifestation in visible form of this Divine Life, and as far as you let It, It will show forth in and through you according to Its basic nature. Its nature is perfection; perfection in life and in substance. And you can insure Its showing forth this perfection-nature by working in harmony with It, by doing your part consistently of this mutual work. You are of the royal household, but unless you live your life royally in every respect, this will be true only potentially. Every inharmony which you have ever experienced has come into your life through one or another of the misadjustments which we have considered. You now know all the possible causes of disease, and you know that sickness is simply that faulty functioning resulting from disobedience to law. You know that healing is readjustment and that when complete readjustment has been made, there is no longer any root to nourish inharmony.

The next step in demonstrating the truth about yourself is to begin to extend this knowledge of your own nature and of the unreality of disease as a positive, malignant force, into your subconsciousness. Make your body easy, and with your eyes closed concentrate your attention on your hands. Feel the warmth and the minute vibration in them. That is your life. Carry this exploration into the various parts of your body — feet, abdomen, neck, head. You will not find the vibratory evidence of your life equally strong in all the tissues, but with practice and concentration you will be able to recognize yourself, your life, throughout your body. Now, with your attention still directed within, repeat this affirmation:

Thou in me art vibrant and regenerating health, and I am now perfect in every cell and fiber, in every function and activity.

Remember that this has always been the 'potential truth about yourself and that all that has hindered it from expressing itself perfectly through you was your ignorant or wilful violation of the laws of righteous living. Now that you have done away with this and so have come into harmony with your true nature, that nature is certain to manifest itself. You have made the cause right, and the result is bound to follow.

As you use this affirmation, let your attention take in, from time to time, the various parts of your body. You are speaking directly to your life in your tissues, are reminding it of something it has forgotten. It is Infinite Life, but it has taken on the limitations of the race. Now you are getting back to the truth about yourself, and this awakening of the vitality to a knowledge of itself is a very important step.

Remember that before the various phenomena of healing and immunity, the so-called "scientists" have long been filled with wonder. They have experimented with the crudest methods for arousing this regenerating activity of the inner life, but now you are dealing direct with Life, your own life and at the same time the Father's. By your three-fold readjustments, you are removing every hindrance to the cleansing and regenerating process.

Now let us suppose that you are manifesting certain "symptoms" of disease. What are you to do with them? You are to turn the full voltage of the Father's life upon them, realizing that this life, which built your body in the first place, is abundantly able and willing to rebuild it now. A "symptom of disease" is simply an indication of inharmony in thinking, feeling, or acting. You have made part of these causes right; your belief in disease is the last thing to go, and you are now destroying that.

You may find this formula of assistance in destroying false beliefs: Turning directly upon the troublesome symptom, repeat silently but earnestly:

Weakness, discomfort, and pain are delusions: thy life in me is radiant health, harmonious power.

If your trouble has been diagnosed by a physician or by your well-meaning friends, you may find it necessary to deal with the name given it. Here is one way of tearing down this rubbish of false belief in organized evil:

Consumption is a lie: thou art the reality of my life and body, and thou art perfect.

For the word "consumption" substitute any other that you may desire to eliminate from your consciousness.

There exists in your subconsciousness an idea-pattern of yourself as performing certain actions, or expressing yourself in certain ways; if you are "sick," you have unconsciously accepted the ideal of sickness, and in your subconsciousness you regard yourself as doing everything from the invalid's standpoint. You must reverse this. Use your visualizing power to see yourself doing the work that you want to do, and doing it masterfully and joyously. Build a rosary of words descriptive of this real nature. Say, "I am vigorous, masterful, joyous, vibrant with life and energy; my eyes are bright, my skin pink and wholesome. I breathe deeply, and perform all the functions of life easily and perfectly." Never mind the shadows of appearance — you are getting back to the cause realm now, and for the present you have no concern with results. They will right themselves presently. And remember, this is not simply dogmatic faith. It is reasonable and logical, and is bound to work. You are not asking to be forgiven for continued violation of law, but are building new and eternal health on a basis of self-knowledge and self-mastery. You have insured this health you are claiming by readjusting your habits, physical, mental, emotional.

If you have a particularly troublesome "remembrance" of the old way of living, in the form of a physical symptom which seems to resist the healing vibrations, remember, first, that the real root of the trouble is within; you have not yet succeeded in freeing your mind from all belief in disease as a sinister and positive power, have not yet fully comprehended that it is the logical result of your own creative power used unscientifically. As the next step in demonstrating freedom from this symptom, you may do one of two apparently contradictory things:

First, you may deny this symptom; deny its reality and its power over you, whenever it strikes to call itself to your attention. Call it by name, in the way illustrated in the formula dealing with "consumption" above. Call it a liar, a deceiver. Say, "Get thee behind me, Satan, for thou savorest not of the things that are of God!" God is the one, eternal truth, and He is not subject to imperfection. Your real nature is His nature, and now you are actualizing this possibility by claiming it and living in harmony with its conditions. Disease for you has come to be a lie, and you can meet it firmly with this consideration and statement. This is a very effective form of treatment.

Or, second, you may utilize the "laying on of hands." Your own hand will do. Rest it lightly on the troublesome part, or over it. Accompany this with a silent and wordless contemplation of the real nature of these tissues: see them luminous and radiant with Divine Life. Realize that they are formed out of the Divine Substance, and have in them always and eternally the potentialities of the Father Himself. They are not subject to imperfection except as you, through your misuse of your power as the Son of God, have created the temporary appearance of disease in them.

This laying on of hands enables you very effectually to concentrate your attention on any part of your body. Sometimes the immediate effect is to cause a reddening of the part treated, and even to increase soreness and pain. Pain is always a manifestation of life, however, and increased pain often means quickened healing. In utilizing the laying on of hands, you may either visualize or affirm or both. See the tissues radiant with Divine Life; affirm wholeness and perfection.

Perhaps the best practice in regard to symptoms may be summed up in this way: Never heed a symptom unless it becomes troublesome, and then do not examine it to see what it indicates, how bad or unfavorable it is; never deal with symptoms in a negative or receptive attitude of mind — never accept them at their own apparent valuation. When it is necessary to deal directly with symptoms, look fully at them with the inner vision and speak the word of truth and healing to them. At other times, ignore them absolutely. If you form the habit of "pulling yourself up by the roots" at frequent intervals to see how you are progressing, you will delay healing greatly. Make all the necessary readjustments to bring you into harmony with the law, then accept your innate and natural health and go about your work.

Healing by readjustment and affirmation deals with solid and apparently resistant "matter," and with a mysterious and hidden "vitality." Beyond this form of healing lies that master-method which has been used from time to time by the world's prophets and seers — the method of transformation. Such healing is based on the truth about life and substance: that they are basically divine and have always within them the divine potentialities. Most of the healing of New Thought is effected by the process of growth, in which right conditions and ideals are furnished as a sort of matrix for the rebuilding of the body. Transformation, on the other hand, does its work instantly; it goes back of the secondary causes of Nature, and deals with the life and substance of the Father at first hand. This was the method of Jesus.

Because we accept the race belief in the solidity and resistance of flesh, our healing, or the healing effected through our consciousness, is slow and imperfect. We believe that the physical body must be rebuilt cell by cell. Jesus knew that flesh was but a manifestation of Divine Substance, and was therefore fluid and pliant before the perfecting vision of the Christ mind. Therefore he said, "Be thou whole" and it was so instantly.

The theory of "natural" health and immunity accepts the resistance by the bodily forces to all sinister influences; the ultimate truth is that there are no sinister influences, that all force is good, but that sometimes it has lost its way, does not know itself any more than does unregenerate man. This is the reason for the efficiency of the statement so often used by the Nazarene: "Thy sins are forgiven thee!" There is but one basic sin, out of which all the others have sprung: that is the sin of ignorance, which leads man to believe in separation from Good. Jesus constantly used his dissolving and transmuting power to free men from belief in separation from Good and in subjection to "evil." He did not often teach the outer man, for the time for such teaching was not yet come — any more than it is fully come now; but He freed the subconsciousness, for the time, from its belief in sickness and evil.

The full healing realization which is expressed in this statement, "Thy sins are forgiven thee," is this: "In life and substance you are an expression of the Father, and are therefore perfect. God is the all-in-all of your life and body, and God is not subject to limitation or evil. From my own Christ consciousness, I now free your lower mind from its belief in these things, and restore to you your own wholeness and perfection."

The limitation inherent in this form of healing is that, while it can instantly change the entire bodily chemistry, can transform and regenerate wasted tissue, and can rebuild defective organs, even the master who uses it can do no more to change the thoughts and desires of others than to caution them to "go and sin no more." Therefore it has a tendency to eliminate that course of education in thought, action, and emotion which the gradual conquering of the false mode of expression called "disease" brings. Sickness is educative. It indicates always a lack of adjustment between the individual and his divine source, and before the results of this misadjustment can be permanently removed, the cause must be made right.

In explaining even briefly the form of spiritual healing which I have called "transformation," it will be necessary to get back again to the old ideal of love. Love is the real healing power; and the higher the form of healing, the more must it partake of the love nature. Transformation is based on love, the essential lovingness of divine life and substance, wherever found. It is through this basic love quality that you are to manifest control, for perfect love within you harmonizes with perfect love throughout the universe, and makes your oneness with all life real and active instead of merely potential. The love that is in your consciousness, love for all things, great and small, speaks to the latent love in all things and makes them responsive to your will. Even the sinister "bacterium" will obey you if you speak from this love center. But to be able to heal in this way, you must live love and think love toward all life and substance, at all times, and not merely when you are desirous of demonstrating healing.

In the work of changing an undesirable manifestation of any kind to an ideal condition, your attitude must be not that of destroying evil, but of transforming it. This is supremely important, for it is absolutely impossible to destroy anything. To take the mental attitude of attempting to destroy that which is a part of the Father, is to place yourself in opposition to, and so in [inharmony with, the Father's life. By recognizing the innate divinity of both life and flesh, you call forth, through your expectant recognition of the truth, that divinity. In doing away with pestilence or plague, you are merely a "seer," one who beholds the truth, and who, by recognizing it from the inner plane of consciousness, brings it into outer manifestation. A correct understanding of this principle of transformation is of the highest importance, for transformation is normal and is easily accomplished through a knowledge of the law, while destruction is impossible.

This manner of healing through transformation is "strong meat," and many of my readers will not yet be ready for it. For those who are able to grasp its real significance, I will add a few words of advice. Remember always that spiritual mastery is a part of spiritual living — it cannot be exercised by him whose motives are selfish or whose life is intermittently given over to sensual delusions. The resistance to your word of command is not in Nature, but in yourself. Until you fully recognize your own divinity, which you can do only by living the divine life in every detail, Nature will not recognize you as master.

Love is the real healing power, for it is love that brings the finite and the infinite together; if you fail in healing, get down to business and bring out your love faculty. Remember that the inductive power of your emotions has great effect on lower forms of life. The mere belief that they are hostile, the attitude of resistance and fear, makes them take on a sinister appearance.

Do not hold yourself separate in consciousness from the form and energy which you desire to transform — it is through your oneness of life and substance, first, with the Father, and second, with all other manifestations of Him, however unattractive, that you are able to speak the word of transformation. The attitude of mind which strives to change something entirely separate from and outside of itself insures failure.

In your first attempts to heal by your word of transformation, consider very fully the theory upon which such healing is based. Turn your attention upon the patient, and with serene love and trust speak to the Father's consciousness and substance in his tissues. Remember that he is a manifestation of the Father and that from your own Christ consciousness you can speak to the divine within him. You can use this realizing formula:

Father, I thank thee that thou hearest me and that even now thou dost manifest thyself, thy life and substance, clean and strong and perfect in these parts.

See the parts perfect, if you can; if not, hold to the realization, forcing yourself to remember and consider the logic of your treatment. After you have done this for a few minutes, drop the matter from your mind entirely — don't keep "nagging," but rather take your mind off the subject and trust the Father to do His part of the work. If you will do this, and will live consistently, you will find that as you learn to concentrate more and more perfectly and confidently on the work you are doing, the time required for perfect transformation or healing will grow less and less, until results will come instantly.

In this volume, I have striven to help my readers find that way of masterful living, in feeling, thinking, and acting, which, when consistently followed, insures mastery. You were created for success: for that full and all-comprehending success of which health and joy and abundance are but parts. Masterful living is normal to you, but as long as you persist in looking to the symbol, in the formed world, for power and wisdom, you will not show forth this mastery. The key lies in your own heart.

The Kingdom is there, and the way to this Kingdom, though straight and narrow, requires but earnestness and humbleness from those who are to follow it successfully. Learn to look within for the divinity which shall bring you peace and abundance; learn to see divinity in all without. That is the whole secret of righteousness and its consequent mastery.

THE END.

Made in the USA
Middletown, DE
23 September 2022

11086208R00055